INNOVATIVE TRENDS IN PERSONALIZED SOFTWARE ENGINEERING AND INFORMATION SYSTEMS

Frontiers in Artificial Intelligence and Applications

The book series Frontiers in Artificial Intelligence and Applications (FAIA) covers all aspects of theoretical and applied Artificial Intelligence research in the form of monographs, selected doctoral dissertations, handbooks and proceedings volumes. The FAIA series contains several sub-series, including 'Information Modelling and Knowledge Bases' and 'Knowledge-Based Intelligent Engineering Systems'. It also includes the biennial European Conference on Artificial Intelligence (ECAI) proceedings volumes, and other EurAI (European Association for Artificial Intelligence, formerly ECCAI) sponsored publications. The series has become a highly visible platform for the publication and dissemination of original research in this field. Volumes are selected for inclusion by an international editorial board of well-known scholars in the field of AI. All contributions to the volumes in the series have been peer reviewed.

The FAIA series is indexed in ACM Digital Library; DBLP; EI Compendex; Google Scholar; Scopus; Web of Science: Conference Proceedings Citation Index – Science (CPCI-S) and Book Citation Index – Science (BKCI-S); Zentralblatt MATH.

Volume 324

Recently published in this series

ISSN 0922-6389 (print)
ISSN 1879-8314 (online)

Innovative Trends in Personalized Software Engineering and Information Systems

The Case of Intelligent and Adaptive E-learning Systems

By

Christos Troussas

Department of Informatics and Computer Engineering, University of West Attica, Greece

and

Cleo Sgouropoulou

Department of Informatics and Computer Engineering, University of West Attica, Greece

Press

Amsterdam • Berlin • Washington, DC

ISBN 978-1-64368-096-5 (print)
ISBN 978-1-64368-097-2 (online)
Library of Congress Control Number: 2020941145
doi: 10.3233/FAIA324

Publisher
IOS Press BV
Nieuwe Hemweg 6B
1013 BG Amsterdam
Netherlands
fax: +31 20 687 0019
e-mail: order@iospress.nl

For book sales in the USA and Canada:
IOS Press, Inc.
6751 Tepper Drive
Clifton, VA 20124
USA
Tel.: +1 703 830 6300
Fax: +1 703 830 2300
sales@iospress.com

Foreword

Knowledge-based systems refer to computer programs that reason and use a knowledge base to solve complex problems and are an area of high interest by researchers. The attempt of these systems to represent knowledge explicitly allowing the emergence of new knowledge as well as the ever-increasing need of software to become even more individualized and adaptive to users' needs and preferences can illustrate the motivation of the authors to explore this area. Christos Troussas and Cleo Sgouropoulou analyzed the case of intelligent and adaptive learning technology systems. In the light of new advancements in knowledge-based software engineering, the authors conducted a detailed research and worked towards addressing the resulting obstacles giving potential and robustness to the modern ways of e-learning through the incorporation of artificial intelligence and knowledge-based approaches.

This book explores several complex and sophisticated techniques that are used by e-learning software to build an individualized learning environment and offer a student-centric experience to the users. On top of that, the authors research evaluation models and frameworks that are tailored to assess the quality and effectiveness of knowledge-based systems.

Considering the above, I strongly believe that the authors made admirable effort to further explore this important research field and this monograph is a significant contribution to the pertinent literature. This book can be a valuable tool for junior and senior researchers as well as software developers that seek to implement learning technology systems of improved quality in terms of adaptivity and intelligence.

Athens, Greece

Prof.-Dr. Ioannis Voyiatzis
University of West Attica

Contents

Chapter 1: Introduction

Many educational organizations and university institutions use e-learning means to provide the required training to their students according to their own time commitments or obligations. In recent years, e-learning has undergone a major change in the provision of education, allowing trainees to access educational material at any time and from any place they wish. In such contexts, trainers and trainees may live in different locations and never meet each other in person in a real-class environment, except in a virtual learning environment (Sharma et al., 2010). As such, many educational interventions that appear in the literature are related exclusively to educational design and the goals they expect to achieve. In general, they mainly lack the incorporation and integration of intelligent approaches yet (Alharbi and Jemmali, 2017).

For example, one of the first differences in traditional practice concerned the flow of educational design. It is not enough just to digitize the process and transfer it to the electronic contexts as there is no differentiation regarding conventional education. A major gap identified in this issue was the possible existence of a smart and dynamic flow for educational design that will change its content depending on the needs and preferences of each user (Wilson et al., 2007).

Another point is the possibility of adapting the educational systems according to each trainee, since each one learns in his own way and pace. However, in order to be able to develop such intelligent and adaptive systems, it is crucial to find the educational needs of the users. A key point is the ability to create user profiles as well as student models that are the result of study and analysis, knowledge, skills and personality of students.

This book highlights the knowledge-based techniques and the novelties that can be applied in e-learning systems, as well as the benefits emerging from appropriate educational design by incorporating intelligent systems, in order to achieve better learning outcomes as well as greater student satisfaction and engagement during the educational process.

1.1   Artificial Intelligence as a Paradigm

It is not easy to define the term Artificial Intelligence (AI). But let's try to use some historical definitions to determine the scientific field of Artificial Intelligence.

John McCarthy[1] was the first to define the term Artificial Intelligence in 1955. In particular, he stated that "the goal of Artificial Intelligence is to develop machines that behave as if they were intelligent". This definition can be further expanded by enriching it with the notion that AI can offer solutions to practical problems that are more demanding than simple paradigms of intelligent machines, such as Braitenberg vehicles (Rano, 2014).

---

[1] https://www.artificial-solutions.com/blog/homage-to-john-mccarthy-the-father-of-artificial-intelligence

Other definitions state that AI is the ability of digital computers or computer-controlled robots to solve problems that are normally associated with the highest cognitive processing capabilities of humans". According to the above definition, any computer that could, for example, quickly perform a multiplication of two numbers consisting of 20 digits, could be treated as an Artificial Intelligence system; such a consideration cannot figure the concepts of AI.

According to definition of AI by Elaine Rich (1983), "Artificial Intelligence is the study of how we create computers that will do things that people are better at right now". With the above short and straightforward definition, it is explained what researchers in the field of Artificial Intelligence have been doing for the last 50 years and what they will continue to do for the next years.

In terms of computing power and the ability to calculate complex operations in a short period of time, digital computers have outgrown humans since their early stages. However, there are many areas in which man is far ahead. An example of this could be recognizing an unfamiliar environment and making decisions about it in fractions of a second, which is extremely demanding for a machine to conduct until now. It is understood that, according to Rich's definition, the above example is a field of application of Artificial Intelligence.

However, it would not be appropriate to assume that Artificial Intelligence deals exclusively with the dogmatic application of intelligent processes. According to Rich's definition, intelligent systems cannot be created without a deep understanding of human logic and intelligence, which is why neuroscience has made the greatest contribution to the development of Artificial Intelligence.

One of the most important features of human intelligence is adaptability. The ability of people to adapt to different environmental conditions and the corresponding change in their behavior is achieved through the learning process. Precisely because in the possibility of learning, man is superior to the state of machines, machine learning is one of the most basic subcategories of Artificial Intelligence. Thus, after years of research on neural networks, very important scientific achievements have emerged (Troussas et al., 2020 (a)). One such example is the use of very powerful deep learning networks to categorize high-precision images, an application which is extremely important for all types of intelligent systems. In practice, this application was the trigger for the start of the Artificial Intelligence Revolution, which led to the development of self-driving vehicles and other smart machines.

1.2   E-learning

There are two main forms of learning, the traditional form (presentation in the physical classroom) and the electronic form (electronic computer learning). In recent years, there has been a differentiation and transfer of the way of education to more modern ways. Conventional and traditional environments have begun to be transformed into electronic classrooms and learning to take place in virtual environments. E-learning is gaining more and more ground in the field of education (Chen and Yen, 1998). It is also argued that e-learning can be a solution, or a tool for supporting lifelong learning.
Under this rationale, e-learning technology has been accepted by many educational institutions and organizations. This has been done since it is an increasing interest of

people to render education accessible to anyone, anytime, anywhere.

There are several bibliographic definitions for e-learning that define it mainly as the means by which education and training are provided. Most definitions focus on content access and not program results. Some of these definitions are:

- E-learning is defined as the provision of education (of any form and of any relationship in terms of training and education) through various electronic multimedia (Koohang and Harman, 2005).
- E-learning is a process with digital tools and content that may require some interactivity and there may be an interaction between instructor-learner-stakeholders.
- E-learning is defined as the use of new multimedia technology and the Internet to improve the quality of education, giving access to different sources and content, as well as remote communication and collaboration (Alonso et al., 2005).

Taking into consideration the above, the following concept is more concise:

- E-learning is defined as a modern approach of training or education, which incorporates all the necessary elements of educational design, and is based on the use of electronic multimedia material, tools and devices aimed at improving access to education, communication and interaction, by anyone, anytime, anywhere, and which embraces a new way of understanding and development of learning. (Sangrà et al., 2012)

The use of e-learning can give many advantages to the educational process, some of which are the following:

- E-learning can help people with learning disabilities or people with special needs who cannot attend lectures in physical classrooms. (Zhou et al., 2008)
- The fact that e-learning is a research area of high interest means that existing tools and practices from formal education are usually used, thus enabling the testing of additional systems that can support the learning process. (Zhou et al., 2008).

1.3   AI in Education

During the years of developing e-learning software, many research efforts have been made to support it with various systems and tools (Troussas et al., 2019 (a); Troussas et al., 2019 (b)). Indicatively, the combination of all these tools aims to achieve better learning outcomes, better learning experience for the user as well as a personalized learning experience depending on the characteristics of each learner.

Adaptive educational environments emphasize the importance of learning differentiation through educational platforms. Recognizing and delivering learners' traits is a very important part of the success of these systems. In order to be able to make efficient use of these systems, it is necessary to record the characteristics of the learners and to pay special attention to the study and analysis of these data. (Shute and Zapata-Rivera, 2012).

Applying artificial intelligence to education has been a major challenge in recent years. It includes the integration of principles, rules, theories of psychology, etc. in this field. The main goal is to provide systems and software that can be used in the educational process and to support it in a more effective way. Using such techniques, smart systems can be created that will model students in an intelligent way (Greer, 1995).

Smart systems are based on knowledge and are intended to mimic the learner's thinking. To achieve this goal, they use techniques such as machine learning, knowledge engineering, virtual reality, etc. (Salem, 2010).

Chapter 2:
Intelligent Knowledge-Based Approaches for Adaptive and Personalized Learning Technology Systems

Educational software based on artificial intelligence techniques adapts learning to the individual needs of learners, brings them into direct contact with each other, provides access to digital material and supports education decentralization. The application of this new technology to human learning requires deep knowledge in the field of the educational design and assessment as well. Artificial intelligence techniques are necessary for the development of perceptions and knowledge, for the provision of a rich assessment of how people learn and for the measurement of students' collective activity.

Machine learning and data mining methods are used to discover educational data and to understand students as well as their needs, preferences, strengths and weaknesses (Troussas et al., 2020 (b)). Artificial intelligence provides tools for developing computational models to distinguish the aforementioned aspects. In addition, artificial intelligence methods can reform learning environments to provide knowledge about the domain to be learned and teaching strategies through cognitive and emotional modeling, questions and answers in natural language, and machine learning methods.

2.1   AI Systems and Techniques

2.1.1   Intelligent Architecture for E-learning System

A large part of the research that is conducted in the field of educational design concerns the flow of processes and how they can become individualized according to the needs of each user (Alharbi and Mahdi, 2017). Following, an intelligent tutoring architecture is presented that changes according to the needs of each user, but is also supports systems being able to predict the interests and preferences of learners. Another important element of this architecture is the ability to filter electronic sources that will be useful exclusively to the user, while blocking any unrelated content.

A brief presentation is presented, as follows:
- Modeling the user: the user of the application can provide information about his/her interests. These can change over time depending on his preferences. It also contains basic personal information.
- Feedback delivery: The purpose is to inform the user with the delivery of messages. Messages are created through the management of data of the Filtering and Intelligent components.
- Smart agent: In order the system to be able to deliver response to students, they should begin to have some interaction with it. In addition, Intelligent components can be based on the interaction activity of other similar users with common

profile features. In more detail, the network learns through user handling and transmits this information to the Creator. In addition, through the understanding of the user's behavior, it can also provide information to the e-resource for the provision of relevant material to the user. Through the feedback points there are additional elements that we keep for the user's profile and are forwarded to the Feedback delivery to personalize the material of each user.

- Collector: It supports the collection of electronic material from various sources and supports the Filtering component by providing digital content.
- Refining: The main use of this element is to filter the material. Its purpose is to provide solely new material that the user has not used before; the content that has been already used by the students is not presented to him/her. Also, its main advantage is the possibility to prevent the presentation of the same content to the user.
- User interface: It refers to the environment in which the user interacts with the system. This includes environments in any electronic device. Through this element the user configures his/her profile and gives the necessary feedback to the system.

2.1.2   Bayesian Probability

In probability theory and statistics, the Bayes' theorem describes the probability of an event, based on prior knowledge of conditions that may be related to the event.

The approach of this theory was modeled in order to detect knowledge in educational software and analyze whether it can be predicted for a specific student (Firte et al., 2009). Namely, depending on his/her previous knowledge, it is possible that s/he will understand a part of what is going to be taught to him. This approach can greatly support the structure of an educational software that will be based on the capabilities of a particular student. This technique is applied quite often to situations where it is important to predict the future knowledge acquisition levels of a student depending on his/her current performance. Therefore, the software can be able to deal with any knowledge gaps that one may have and to cover them with more different learning material. The problem in applying this theory is the parameter values and the parameters themselves. Factors that affect the configuration option are the learning object, the level, the platform, etc. The Bayesian method is appropriate towards providing a mechanism for combining information observations with previous information and generating a probability distribution sample for parameters such as a students' skills related to performance criteria by grades. In summary, an educational software will accept as an entry the previous knowledge and performance of a student on a specific topic/lesson and in combination with the correlation of this knowledge with the new one, it is able to predict whether the student can meet success in assessments. The reason why Bayesian Probability is used is to render the student able to move on to the next level in a lesson only when s/he is ready for it in terms of cognitive abilities and will not have significant gaps that may delay his/her performance or confuse him/her. Each person learns at his/her own pace, so it is important to adapt to him/her without following predetermined learning paths and towards having the best results in learning.

The existing knowledge of a student is introduced in the software and according to the Bayes' theorem, the conclusion is drawn about whether the student will be able to correctly understand what is to follow.

This technology will help teachers to check if there are serious knowledge gaps in students that prevent them from advancing their knowledge.

2.1.3   Learning Analytics

Learning analytics is the measurement, collection, analysis and reporting of data about students and the learning environment in order to understand and optimize the educational process and the contexts in which it occurs.

Analysis is the process of adding information to data using algorithmic techniques. Decision making is an important goal of any learning process. The results of the monitoring activity will determine the success or failure of Learning Analytics. This process is based on a set of mathematical and statistical algorithms known as machine learning techniques. The most advanced learning analytics algorithms lead to better knowledge. However, complex algorithms impose high demands on the collected data in terms of their volume, type, collection time frame, etc.

As a result of learning analytics, two types of educational process analysis can be obtained. The first is the detailed descriptive learning elements. These types of analysis are reactive. They allow the understanding of the past activity and based on this knowledge they predict the future activity. The second type is the learning predictions. These kinds of analysis are precautionary. They affect the present activity and therefore they improve the ongoing learning processes. The dividing line between descriptive and predictive analysis can be crossed with correct data and appropriate algorithms. Choosing the appropriate data and algorithms is vital to properly implement learning analysis processes.

Researchers in the field of learning analytics analyze a variety of learning systems (Krouska et al., 2019 (a)), such as content management systems. The main concern is to maintain the knowledge and performance of the learners and the results of their assessments. The large amount of data can be drawn from previous student performance in various teaching methods or learning content that will be considered as data for a particular knowledge level of the students. So, through the abundance of data, educational software can figure out the already existing knowledge of a single learner or group of learners as well as skills and abilities and will provide the appropriate guidance. This process will help teachers to improve the acquisition of knowledge and skills of their students but also to maximize dynamic learning while strengthening teaching and tutoring methods. Having integrated learning analytics into educational software, this, in turn, can analyze how each student learns and present these findings to the instructors who will use them to facilitate the student.

The software accepts as input a large amount of data related to previous performance, skills and abilities of the trainees. After the processing, which is based on mathematical and statistical algorithms, multiple conclusions are drawn for each learner individually.

There are three reasons why learning analytics is used in educational software. Performance maintenance is increasing. Detailed learning data can be used to reduce drop-out rates and increase student performance. Content and learning quality are improved. Learning analytics can be used to recognize patterns of content utilization, understand content quality issues and offer a personalized learning experience to students, the so-called adaptive learning. Learning analytics can be used to identify and promote success factors as well as to understand the path of students advancing their knowledge in an educational program; this facilitates the design of a curriculum that will be developed through an educational software.

2.1.4   Data Mining

Data mining is about finding new information through existing data. Data form processed information can be used in conjunction with new inputted information for further knowledge extraction.

Data is the key element of analysis and can be seen as the raw material that is transformed into analytical knowledge. The data collected for educational purposes can be seen as information sets, being collected from students, learning environment, learning interactions and learning outcomes. This information is collected during the learning process. The data can come from demographic and academic sources, student activity files, student performance information. The data and mining techniques involve machine learning techniques and analytical algorithms.

One of the main goals of educational software is to evaluate and enhance the educational processes. Mining is the process of searching for hidden information from a large amount of data. It analyzes data from different sources and converts it into important and valuable information. Utilizing data mining techniques in education is a research field of growing interest, which deals with the development of methods that assist the discovery of specific data types emerged from the educational environment (Repčíková, 2013; Troussas et al., 2013). The main goal is to acquire new learning techniques and to upgrade the academic results. Various ways of classifying, grouping and correlating are used to enhance students' performance, time management for their education and course selection.

Data mining in education focuses on developing methods to discover educational data involving the understanding the learning process of learners and the tutoring methods they prefer. Learner activity with the educational software can be rich in content. Data that refer to this interaction is the level of answers in questions, the session of educational software with the student, his/her level of knowledge, the level of knowledge of an entire class, etc. Another use of data mining is to monitor and predict the progress of learners at all levels of learning. Data mining can also support the feedback to students and their cognitive development while interacting with educational software, the available courses, etc. Data mining helps to predict students' final grades in exams and determine their performance. It is also used to keep student records in the educational systems.

Finally, the methodology used to develop learning management systems does not hold intelligent techniques yet, namely when the processing of a course is completed and published, it cannot be modified again. Through data mining, a dynamic processing methodology can emerge, where useful information will be discovered to improve the educational process. Data mining can support the student as well as develop the quality of educational software.

The large amount of data and its collection is a vital point for most artificial intelligence applications. It is very important to use all the available information. The main use of information, derived from data mining, is to predict performance and highlight misconceptions or problems in order to prevent or correct them.

2.1.5   Machine Learning

Machine learning is an integral part of artificial intelligence that provides systems with the ability to automatically learn and improve from experience without explicit planning. These systems have access to data that they use to train themselves.

Machine learning techniques have proven to be useful tools in any kind of software including educational systems (Bhutto et al., 2020; Virvou et al., 2012). Their ability to repeatedly observe how learners learn and react to the system leads to the creation of "rules" for them. Another use of these techniques is to improve user models and even user groups in quantity and quality. Systems that use machine learning can observe the behavior of previous learners and provide paradigms that are a reference point for predicting future actions by other learners. The groups of users that are formed are classified according to individual patterns with common interests, knowledge and skills. The educational software that uses such techniques acquires new knowledge for the learners and the groups in which they are clustered and predicts the degree of influence in the learning process. Instructors who choose to incorporate techniques of this category promote the adaptivity of the learning environment to students and use the new data to make better decisions about the course. Student performance is predicted using the acquired knowledge for each student; machine learning models can then discover students' weaknesses and suggest ways to improve. Teachers and students are constantly provided with feedback on how students learn, the support they need, and the progress they are making towards achieving their goals. The retention rate is improving. By identifying possible errors, educational software can identify students who need more assistance and maintain a satisfactory pace of learning throughout their interaction with the system. As such, teachers can be significantly supported. Effectiveness can increase because machine learning has the potential to render teachers capable of completing tasks such as domain delivery planning. In turn, teachers can focus on tasks that cannot be accomplished by computers and require human intervention. Machine learning can also help teachers gain knowledge that cannot be collected using human brain. Therefore, computers can make deep dives into data, analyze content and make connections and conclusions that positively affect the teaching and learning process. Machine learning, as the form of predictive analysis, can draw conclusions about things that may happen in the future. For example, using a set of data from high school students' summary files, analytical forecasting methods can predict who is more likely to drop out due to academic failure or even his/her score on a standardized test. Machine learning can offer adaptive education to students who either have advanced or poor knowledge and as such they want different handling. Adaptive learning software is a technological or electronic educational system that analyzes students' performance in real time and modifies teaching methods and curriculum based on this data. Individualized learning can then be used to give each student a personalized educational experience. Personalized learning is an educational experience where students guide their own learning, go at their own pace and, in some cases, make their own decisions about what they need to learn. Ideally, in a classroom that uses personalized learning, students choose material based on their interests and teachers match the curriculum and standards with the students' needs. Moreover, machine learning can used to rate students' assignments and examinations more accurately than humans can. It may take a while for a person to make input of data, but the results will be more valid and reliable.

Through the monitoring of procedures, such as the response of students to the software, evaluation, performance, etc. the software starts can realize how the educational process works and creates patterns that are followed and reformed without the need for human intervention.

Through these patterns, the software can predict and prevent situations, make general predictions about learners and their performance, and help the design of a personalized learning experience for each learner.

2.1.6   Genetic Algorithms

Genetic algorithms are adaptive search algorithms inspired by Darwin's theory of evolution[1]. A number of potential solutions to an optimization problem are evolving into better solutions according to the principles of heredity, mutation, natural selection and recombination.

Genetic algorithms have been shown to be a useful technique for optimizing learning applications but also for recognizing a student's form of learning (Krouska et al., 2019 (b); Krouska et al., 2020). The advantages of using genetic algorithms in recognizing forms of learning are two-fold. First, genetic algorithms are an effective method for investigating a wide range of forms to determine the combination preferred by a student. Second, these algorithms are able to adapt to changing conditions when searching, because a student perceives and processes information in a way that can change over time, and educational systems should be able to adapt their behavior to the alterations of learning modes. Genetic algorithms aim to detect the combination of actions that the student performs normally while studying the material delivered by an educational software. It is necessary to observe the interaction of students with the educational software in different phases of this interaction. Then, the combination of the observed actions will be considered as the combination of actions that the student prefers and is mapped in some form of learning.

Genetic algorithms are similar to statistical data, as the form of the model must be known in advance. Genetic algorithms use selection, crossover, and mutation operators to develop successful solutions. Adaptive search algorithms are applied through the tracking of an learner›s action in an educational software to optimize problems that the learner is experiencing during the learning process. This technique is used to identify a learner›s form of learning and the changes that may occur in it over time.

2.1.7   Pattern Recognition

Pattern recognition is the ability to detect settings, features, or data that provide information about a particular system or data set. Pattern recognition is considered a subcategory of machine learning.

Pattern recognition has the ability to monitor and reason about the attention of a student during the lesson by analyzing the image of his face through a simple camera. The benefits are that the educational software understands if the material provided to the student seems to be interesting to him/her and attracts his/her attention (Lee et al., 2009). Various pattern recognition approaches are also used to determine the student's

---

[1]   https://www.livescience.com/474-controversy-evolution-works.html

learning modality. Depending on the way a student learns and performs adequately, a system can find the pattern with which a student learns. In addition, a system that uses pattern recognition will be able to predict the time needed by a particular student to complete a lesson through the collection of large volumes of data on his/her features and performance. As mentioned, pattern recognition is considered a subcategory of machine learning. Therefore, machine learning techniques can provide a first step for the extraction of useful information from a large amount of data and the knowledge gain to predict student progress and performance.

By observing the reactions of the students, patterns can be extracted that give important information about them and their preferences. An educational software will have the best possible performance if it is adapted to their needs and preferences.

2.1.8   Deep Learning

Deep learning is a subset of machine learning that includes networks being capable of learning in an unsupervised way from data that is unstructured or unmarked.

Deep learning is a core strategy through which educational software can extract the students' understanding concerning the lessons and their experiences (Yang and Wu, 2019; Wang et al., 2019). However, deep learning can be disrupted if existing learners' interests or background do not offer diversity. As the number of available training data has grown, deep learning is becoming more and more useful. Deep learning models have grown as the infrastructure of e-learning systems for educational purposes has improved. Firstly, a mathematical model is created in order to process performance, learning rates, behaviors and reactions, etc. Then, this model is applied to the educational software. Software can learn from experience and understand the educational process in terms of hierarchy of concepts. Gathering knowledge from experience, the teacher does not need to formally identify all the knowledge the computer needs in order to draw conclusions for students.

By collecting information about the learner and the educational process, data is analyzed in their simpler form so that it is connected and software can understand it as simple structures separately and then as concepts all together. Any software that save notion about its functionality can save valuable time for training it. Modern software that incorporates artificial intelligence has the ability to recognize the whole educational process from the learners' point of view.

2.1.9   Neural Networks

Neural networks are a branch of machine learning, supporting the computer to learn to perform some work by analyzing paradigms. The purpose of a neural network is to learn to recognize patterns through a sample of data. Once the neural network is trained, it can make predictions by identifying similar patterns in future data.

The Neural Network is an interconnected network of artificial neurons. This is a smart unit for knowledge processing being interconnected and working like the human brain. The artificial neural network is a key unit for processing knowledge or information in a smart system. Artificial intelligence neurons are connected to each other and function in the same way as biological neurons. The neural network of intelligent technology is a computational technology based on the human brain with certain human-like abilities. In this smart technology, mathematical functions are shaped as a set of artificial neurons in a computerized brain network. All nodes are connected to each other and each connection is defined by weights. When a node takes any input then that input is multiplied by a specified connection weight. Inside the brain, neurons act as nodes.

The neural network adapts the weights of its various connections using the training samples and tries to find the weights that correspond to the most effective connection between process and knowledge. All of these nodes, such as input nodes, internal nodes, and output nodes, process knowledge to solve educational problems using mathematical calculations of input signals and the weight of connections. Thus, neural networks can be very valuable in educational software.

Neural networks work best when the nature of the data is nonlinear. They can last a long time due to their proliferation. Most neural networks rely on the hidden layer process to perform the summation and constantly adjust the weights until they reach an optimal limit, which then produces some effect. This is the reason why they are used in predicting students' results but also in predicting their preferences.

Neural networks can function as successfully as the human brain in terms of training. Neural networks and the human brain are clearly interconnected in terms of knowledge processing. They are a perfect knowledge processing technology that has the ability to develop smart educational software.

Therefore, the technique of neural networks is an indispensable tool for educational software as they try to mimic the function of the human brain as well as how it analyzes and perceives problems and how it solves them (Chrysafiadi et al., 2019). Neural networks will help to predict performance and develop knowledge that will recognize students' mode of learning, as well as to solve problems that arise during the educational process.

Indeed, learning management systems, as well as web technologies, present educational content whenever needed, ensuring the learner's interaction with the material. In student-centered educational systems, the data collected when users interact with the system, if properly collected and analyzed, can provide important feedback on the educational material and the process being carried out.

2.1.9.1 CeLIP Architecture

With the use of CeLIP (Cesae eLearning Intelligent Player) architecture new principles and tools of the intersection of the field of artificial intelligence and educational design are applied (Mota, 2008). An MLP (Multilayer Perceptron) nervous system is used to predicts the form of the next presentation. This system is designed in the form of levels/layers where, through the combination with the nervous system, it forms the next levels. As a result, a complex graph is formed from the beginning to the end. In the example, the nervous system is the nucleus of the artificial intelligence system.

Initially, the system runs a diagnosis action to determine the structure of the learning objects that will cover the educational unit. This is part of the training program. The choice is made based on the knowledge and skills of the student, in order to understand which learning objects should be presented to him.

The type of activities that make up the chain of subjects is selected using pedagogical parameters (learning method, student performance, etc.). So, in each subsequent step, the system searches for what best suits the learner's profile, performance and choices.

The main points of this educational flow are the modeling of the student, the selection of appropriate educational techniques and the selection of the appropriate educational content that corresponds to the personalized learning outcomes.

2.1.10   Knowledge Reasoning

Smart e-learning systems require the knowledge and expertise of several experienced users of the field to be stored in an information system. This knowledge can then be used by anyone related to the application framework (Karna, 2017). However, this knowledge must be gathered, codified and organized in a specific way. This process is called "knowledge technology". It is the most difficult and time-consuming part of developing a smart e-learning system, with plenty of representation techniques developed for it, such as logic, lists, trees, semantic networks, etc.

These systems consist of three main features:
- Knowledge base, including all the knowledge that exists for a topic.
- Inference engine, analyzing the existing knowledge and giving conclusions.
- User interface, receiving the new data provided by the user to the system.

The aim of these systems is not solely to replace the expert ones in a specific domain, but to provide their knowledge in a broader context. For this reason, there are now more problems to solve and fewer experts on them. So, with these systems more people are expected to develop their knowledge and skills.

2.1.10.1 Reasoning with Cases

Assumptions are defined as a list of characteristics that lead to a particular outcome (Katoua, 2012). A complex hypothesis is a set of sub-hypotheses that structures the strategy for solving a problem (e.g. building an airplane). Recognizing the appropriate case to be used to solve a problem is a matter of the artificial intelligence. This activity includes the definition of the topic and the problem as well as the collection of information about relevant cases by experts in the case.

According to the related research, students can learn more effectively through the use of problem-solving examples and then applying this knowledge in real situations (Krouska et al., 2018). Examples include:
- A multimedia description of the problem.
- A description of the correct strategies to be followed in each case.
- A multimedia explanation of why these strategies are appropriate.
- A list of methods where learners recognize whether they have acted correctly.
- A list of principles that need to be understood in order the learners to act properly.

In the next table, there is a comparison between systems based on the hypothesis and the rules.

Table 1.

Factor	Case-based e-learning	Rule-based e-learning
Knowledge base	Experience	Knowledge mechanism
Knowledge acquisition	Through kinesthetic approaches or experience	Through adaptive mechanisms
Recall	Recalling his/her own experiences	Failing to recall his/her own experiences
Learning	Learning though misconceptions	Failing to learn

2.1.11　Fuzzy Logic

Fuzzy logic emerges as a technique that represents and handles data closer to human logic than other mathematical and logical techniques. Values are no longer accurate, as they become fuzzy, meaning that something may belong to a set in a gradual way, namely the item may appear in the same set but with a different priority depending on the student. In order to represent and handle this form of uncertainty, this logic uses fuzzy sets with elements having a rating scale. On this basis, fuzzy logic allows the calculation and programming of mathematics similar to certain forms of human thought. In educational settings, this is a desirable feature, as the results of the data and their analyzes are related to human characteristics and behavior (Troussas et al., 2020; Krouska et al., 2019 (c)). Proper computational representation makes them more reliable and understandable. This section summarizes the most well-known fuzzy techniques used in e-learning systems. It examines their main features in terms of representation, information management and general application.

2.1.11.1　Fuzzy Logic for Knowledge Acquisition

Fuzzy logic systems after their development have gained great popularity and are used as they can mimic human logic. These systems can be used to figure learners' choices about how to acquire knowledge. They are also used to assess the knowledge of learners as well as learning outcomes.

2.1.11.2　Fuzzy Inference System

A Fuzzy Inference System (FIS) is a system that uses the fuzzy set theory to map out outputs based on inputs. It tries to mimic the reasoning behind the processing of human language to represent decision-making problems, make decisions and act accordingly. An FIS has fuzzy rules to model the problem so as to solve it. These rules are in the IF-THEN form and are repeated to be included in sets. A typical fuzzy rule can be: "if y is A then z is B" where A and B are the fuzzy sets defined in areas y and z respectively. The rule expresses the type of relationship between sets A and B, the member function is $\mu A \rightarrow B(y,z)$. The correct choice of this member function depends on the rules of the proposed logic. The use of FIS rules has the following steps:

- It starts with the process of a fuzzy (uncertain) operation, which activates the rules in the knowledge base through the import body. This process is related to the input data $x = (x_1 \ldots x_n)$, which are not fuzzy, in the corresponding fuzzy sets.
- Then the inference mechanism delivers the decisions based on the rules used. A defuzzification process combines some of the results of these rules to produce a real number vector. This process is a function that converts fuzzy values to certain values. There are several available clarification methods in the literature.

2.1.11.3　Fuzzy Logic for Modeling

Model theory, as a branch of mathematical logic, studies the construction and classification of structures. Different methods and techniques have been introduced to build these structures and fuzzy logic is one of them. Fuzzy modeling is a relatively novel approach to develop system models. It uses language based on fuzzy logic patterns to describe the behavior of systems in a qualitative way. A fuzzy model identifies the system with fuzzy values, which are expressed as fuzzy numbers and have linguistic meanings. The formula is:

$$R_1: \text{ if } x_{11} \text{ is } A_{11} \text{ \& } \ldots x_{1p} \text{ is } A_{1p} \text{ then } y \text{ is } B_1$$

$$R_2: \text{ if } x_{21} \text{ is } A_{21} \text{ \& } \ldots x_{2p} \text{ is } A_{2p} \text{ then } y \text{ is } B_2$$

$$R_r: \text{ if } x_{r1} \text{ is } A_{r1} \text{ \& } \ldots x_{rp} \text{ is } A_{rp} \text{ then } y \text{ is } B_r$$

where p is the number of input values, r is the number of rules, x_j,

$1 \leq j \leq p$ is the j-th input variable, A_{ij}, $1 \leq i \leq r$ is the fuzzy set associated with the j-th input variable in the i-th rule. Also, y is the output variable and B_i the fuzzy set related to the output variable in the i-th rule. These models facilitate the integration of existing knowledge into the system model. At the same time, their knowledge and results can easily be understood by expert people.

2.1.11.4 Fuzzy Logic for Recommendation

Recommendation systems are designed to offer guidance to students. They usually work with multiple users, processing metadata from areas of interest and user profiles. Using this information, the system is able to suggest to a user a collection of learning material $D = (d_1, \ldots, d_n)$, which may be the most relevant according to the user's interests. In order to develop a recommendation system, a way to gather information about users' preferences should be created. These preferences are based on a set of primordial assertions $A = (A_1, \ldots, A_n)$. The validity of each of these assertions can be determined for any object in set D. The representation of an object $d \in D$ is then an evaluation of these assertions for that object $A_j(d)$. This shows the degree to which the assertion A_j is satisfied by d. In this context, object d is considered a fuzzy subset of set A.

2.1.11.5 Fuzzy Ontology

An ontology is a specification of the conceptual understanding of a field. It presents the information used by different types in the hierarchy of an idea. Such ideas are presented as classes with properties and these properties are the objects of the classes. As an ontology is a simplified collection of subjects in a domain concept, it is useful to present the content of e-learning systems and document it. A fuzzy ontology is the specification of an ontology based on fuzzy logic. Specifically, it is a collection $O_F = (I, C, R, F, A)$ where:
- I is the set of atoms (objects), also called cases of concepts and
- C is the set of fuzzy concepts. Each concept is in turn a fuzzy set of cases, $C \in C$, $C: I \rightarrow [0,1]$.
- R is the set of relationships. Each $R \in R$ is a n-th fuzzy relation in the field of entities: $E^n \rightarrow [0,1]$. All entities of fuzzy ontology will be denoted by $E = C \cup I$. A special role is played by the taxonomic relationship $T: E^2 \rightarrow [0,1]$ between all the concepts.

- F is the set of fuzzy relations in the set of entities E and a specific field, contained in D. Each element $F \in F$ is a relation $F: E^{(n-1)} \times P \rightarrow [0,1]$, where $P \in D$.
- A is the set of axioms expressed in an appropriate logical language, i.e. the findings that limit the relationship of concepts, individuals, relationships and functions.

In this specification, any concept or relationship is described by fuzzy logic. Its main advantage is the ability to justify cases that belong to multiple and several categories.

2.1.11.6 Fuzzy Logic for Clustering

Fuzzy grouping is used to create fuzzy models from data, with applications in different fields. In a classic grouping approach, each fact must be classified into a category. With the fuzzy approach, this data can belong to more than one group at a time, with gradual integration into each group. Fuzzy grouping algorithms determine an optimal classification by minimizing the objective operation. This function is based on a grouping pattern. The pattern captures the core of the group and is a representation of the features used to describe the domain. The distance from the center of the group determines the degree of participation in it; the participation increases when the distance from the center of the group decreases. Concerning these algorithms for minimizing distances, most approaches of analytical ambiguity use the optimization of the basic objective function c-mean or a modification of it. Due to the number of groups c, the algorithm is based on minimizing the objective function J,

$$J(U,v) = \sum_{i=1}^{n} \sum_{j=1}^{c} \mu_{ij}^m d_{ij}^2$$

with

$$\mu_{ij} \in [0,1]$$

$$\sum_{j=1}^{c} \mu_{ij} = 1$$

$$\sum_{i=1}^{n} \mu_{ij} < n$$

$$1 < j < c \text{ and } 1 < i < n$$

where $v = \{v_1, v_2, ..., v_c\}$. These groups will be updated later. The $n \times c$ table $U = [\mu_{ij}]$ contains the degree of participation of the member i in the group j and $d_{ij}^2 \equiv d^2(x_i, v_j)$ is the square Euclidean difference. The number m is called the exponential weight. To minimize the objective function, group centers and participation scores are selected so that a high participation of given data is displayed, in patterns close to the corresponding center of a group. The higher the value of m, the less the standards with low participation contribute to the objective operation. These patterns are usually ignored when determining group centers and grades. So, the participation rate for each x_i in the k repetition is calculated and the center of the groups is updated according to the equations

$$\mu_{ij}(k) = \left(\sum_{r=1}^{c} (d_{ij}(k)/d_{ir}(k))^{2/(m-1)}\right)^{-1}$$

$$v_j(k+1) = \sum_{i=1}^{n} \mu_{ij}^m(k)x_i / \sum_{i=1}^{n} \mu_{ij}^m(k)$$

The criterion for stopping the iterative process is

$$\|\mu_{ij}(k+1) - \mu_{ij}(k)\| < \varepsilon \, \forall \, ij$$

or when a number of N repetitions are performed.

During the classification phase, given a x_i pattern, it is classified as a member of group j if

$$\mu_{ij} < \mu_{ik} \, \forall \, i \neq k$$

where the members' grades are calculated according to the above equations.

Chapter 3:
Comparison of Techniques and Good Practices for Adaptive and Personalized Learning Technology Systems

3.1   Introduction

This first part of this section presents the comparison of the aforementioned techniques in two parts for better understanding and for assisting readers to select the appropriate one for confronting specific problems.

3.1.1   Categorization of Techniques Depending on What They Do

Each technique has different abilities, for the correct categorization the following 6 verbs were used:
- PREDICTS
- LEARNS
- ADAPTS
- IMPROVES
- RECOGNIZES
- MONITORS

The following table shows the capabilities of each technique according to the above verbs:

	Predicts	Learns	Adapts	Improves	Recognises	Monitors
Bayesian	•					
Learning Analytics		•				•
Data Mining	•		•			•
Machine Learning	•	•		•		•
Genetic Algorithms			•	•	•	
Pattern Recognition					•	•
Deep Learning		•				
Neural Networks	•	•			•	

Bayesian classification predicts the knowledge that a student will have according to his previous knowledge. Learning analytics monitors and learns how students can learn. Data mining monitors and predicts the progress of students and adapts to its changes. Machine learning learns, improves, monitors and predicts factors related to multiple aspects of the learning process and student performance. Genetic algorithms adapt to and improve from changes in the educational process and manage to recognize the students' form of learning. Pattern recognition recognizes and monitors patterns in student behavior. Deep learning learns by students' behavior and reactions. Neural networks learn, recognize and predict patterns. The predominant functions are prediction, learning and monitoring.

3.1.2   Categorization of Techniques According to their Application in Educational Software

Each technique has a variety of applications within educational software. The applications being identified are:
- The level of knowledge of a student is identified.
- A student's performance is predicted.
- The level of knowledge of a student is maintained.
- The level of knowledge of a student is improved.
- Identify students' preferences.
- Software development and improvement.
- Software personalization to students' strengths/needs.
- Identify a form of learning that a student responds best to.

Based on the analysis of techniques, it is inferred that machine learning can be seen as the dominant technique in terms of its frequency of application. The first reason is that it covers a wide range of areas to be used. The second reason is that it can be seen a broader area and a superset which includes the other presented techniques (being a subset). Machine learning can learn from the educational process and the form of students' learning, improve the way the material being presented, address possible problems, monitor and predict student performance. Finally, it manages to maintain the knowledge level and the progress of a student while being able to evolve and adapt to several changes.

	Knowledge Level Identification	Student Performance Prediction	Knowledge Level Maintenance	Knowledge Level Improvement	Student Preference Identification	Software Improvement	Personalization	Identification of Form of Learning
Bayesian	•	•					•	
Learning Analytics			•	•			•	
Data Mining		•			•	•		
Machine Learning		•	•			•		
Generic Algorithms					•	•		•
Pattern Recognition		•						•
Deep Learning					•			•
Neural Networks		•			•			

3.2   Good Practices

The second part of this section presents good practices for adaptive and personalized learning technology systems are presented.

3.2.1   AI Systems

3.2.1.1   Intelligent Architecture for E-learning System

E-learning is offered to a heterogeneous group of students, having the possibility to learn from any place, at any time and using different devices (e.g. computers, smartphones, tablets, etc.). The effectiveness of e-learning can be improved by assessing student performance, providing feedback to the instructor and providing a reliable system for answering questions by combining artificial intelligence for ameliorating the quality of the functions. Several researchers have proposed a personalization system used in an electronic e-learning system to select educational material based on students' cognitive style, preferences and prior knowledge (Troussas et al., 2019 (c); Meacham et al., 2019). One of the main challenges that researchers face is to develop an effective electronic e-learning system that consider different parameters, such as expanding assessment units' database, learner profiling, pre-processing external sites, discovering knowledge in the web, preserving self-paced learning and effective computer-supported collaboration. Moreover, one issue that remains a hot research topic is the incorporation of personalization techniques in e-learning. In view of the above, creating a proper e-learning architecture to integrate the aforementioned functions and possibilities is a crucial step. Following, several frameworks of e-learning architecture are presented.

Learning Technology Systems Architecture (LTSCA)
This model has six basic components: Learning Entity, Delivery, Evaluation, Coach, Learning Recourse, Learning Records (Isiaka, 2016). The student platform offers a graphical user interface for students. Coach is the cornerstone of this model. It provides the learning material, assessment information, answers to questions, etc. The Delivery component is used to deliver the educational material in an appropriate way using multimedia. The Learning Resource component has a directory of information, which determines what information should be provided to a student. The most important component of this model is the Evaluation component that constantly evaluates student's behavior and progress. Learning records retains the information of the student's profile, his/her current and past information as well as his/her personal and academic information.

Sharable Content Object Reference Model (SCORM)
SCORM architectural reference model is very popular among online learning systems (Pestana Santos, 2018). The additional service proposed in this model is the content management system. The system provider has the flexibility to make the content of the learning material available to the users. It also has an application programming interface adapter, which supports the provision of an application-level interface that is independent of programming languages, providing information using only the web browser.

3.2.1.2   Knowledge Reasoning

Rule-Based E-learning Systems
These systems solve problems by inputting information about the problem and then trying to link it to appropriate rules to solve the problem. However, if the same type of problem is given, the exact same solution will be given to it. As such, a major drawback is that these systems do not learn and do not evolve. There are also cases in which these systems may not return any result if the data being received is outside the design they can analyze. Finally, they are very demanding systems in terms of implementation and maintenance time.

Case-Based E-learning Systems
Case-based systems are the evolution of rule-based systems. Such systems try to analyze the problem, looking for something similar to it through the database, and providing a solution based on examining the similar problems it knows.

In the context of the presentation of the two systems there are some issues that are worth noting, as follows:

- Difficulties in acquiring knowledge: one of the main problems arose from poor knowledge on a subject or even lack in experts in the field. Hence, it is important to maintain any form of knowledge, as experts are not always available to provide their expertise.
- Maintenance difficulties: Systems based on rules require particular difficulty in controlling and converting rules into a modern form while maintaining the relationship with prior knowledge. This is a core difference with case-based systems, changes and additions can be easily made as easily as a simple adding of a user to a system.
- Performance experience: The productivity of a rule-based system is related to how efficiently the information and/or knowledge has been presented or attributed to the system. However, in case-based systems, the system itself can improve its performance as it has memory and handles erroneous performance that it had been detected previously.

3.2.1.3 Fuzzy Logic Techniques

3.2.1.3.1 Fuzzy Inference
Fuzzy inference is applied to e-learning systems to provide data management closer to human reasoning. This is a key feature of these systems, as both tutors and students are not usually experts in data processing and interpretation. One of the first approaches to use fuzzy logic in the modeling of e-learning was in the research of Hawkes et al. (1990). In this research work, a learning environment was proposed to serve an evaluation system. This effort detailed on the fuzziness of information and the ability of fuzzy logic to process it computationally. This innovative approach was enriched several years later (Hawkes et al., 1990). The authors introduced a system, called TAPS, for student assessment, which applies degree-related relevance to language labels with fuzzy logic. This effort proposed a direction to use fuzzy distributions and a set of rules for representing, formulating, and restoring uncertainty in student behavior. Furthermore, a fuzzy logic machine was designed to implement the BSS1 guidance system by Warendorf et al. (1997). This effort

offered improved student learning management based on the aforementioned techniques. Moreover, DEGREE (Barros and Verdejo, 2000) is a system designed to facilitate the extraction of relevant information at various levels. The researchers define variables in a qualitative way and model them with linguistic variables. In this context, they characterize the learning to be a collaborative process. The fuzzy inference process describes the behavior of the group, according to the definition of variables and group rules. Another work presented the DomoSim-TPC system (Redondo et al., 2003) which applied automatic methods that allow tutors to analyze the results of classroom activities. Fuzzy inference is used to draw conclusions about students and their behavior in a collaborative learning environment. The fuzzy connection rules are used in the work of Yu et al. (2001) to clarify the relationships between the different patterns of behavior of a student. The parameters included the number of questions asked, the amount of time spent online, and the number of articles read and published. This processing is performed by modifying the traditional web recordings through the fuzzy approach. In order to represent the evaluation of the teachers, Mihalis and Maria (1995) modeled the students' cognitive level and abilities through the processing and aggregation of group work. Research on other classification-related tasks was conducted by Rasmani et al. (2006). The authors studied the views of experts for the development of a new method for assessing students' academic performance. They applied the data-driven fuzzy rule process, giving a fuzzy inference mechanism and rule induction algorithm. Concept maps are another important element in this context. A new method for their automatic construction is proposed by Bai et al. (2008). It was then applied to many adaptive learning systems. This work uses fuzzy rules and reasoning techniques. As such, maps are constructed and the degree of relevance of the relationships between concepts are evaluated. The main goal was the automated construction of the members' collaboration function and the fuzzy rules for fuzzy grading systems. In (Sue et al. 2004; Tseng et al., 2007), the authors propose a two-phase map construction approach to automatically create a pool of ideas using historical test recordings of instructors. Fuzzy logic appears in the first phase, where it is applied to convert the numerical values of the records into symbolic data. At this stage, the data mining approach is used to find the rules of fuzzy correlation. In the second phase, the authors used multiple rules according to the observations in real learning situations. Indeed, the analysis of students' historical learning files is very important in this context. The work of Tsai et al. (2001) suggested an algorithm for fuzzy extraction and two-phase learning. This algorithm offered teachers the analysis and refinement of data from student files. This algorithm was developed with the theory of fuzzy sets. Finally, a comprehensive architecture for a learning environment is proposed in the study of Monova-Zheleva et al. (2008). Individual learning was supported based on an educational system designed with intelligent rules. A fuzzy inference mechanism was used to apply all the rules in this scenario.

3.2.1.3.2 Fuzzy Logic for Modeling

The use of fuzzy models in the design of e-learning systems has also been considered in the related literature (Troussas et al., 2019 (d); Aajli et al., 2016). There are many approaches to this type. In (Arriaga et al., 2005), the authors proposed different fuzzy configurations for students in order to obtain two ways to evaluate a smart learning system. The relativity of cognitive learning ability is determined by fuzzy sets and rules, which in turn determine and modify fuzzy values. In (Di Lascio et al., 1998), the authors describe a new dynamic model that represents the phases of teaching and guiding users in e-learning multimedia systems. This model is based on an algebraic fuzzy structure focused on cognitive variables. It allows the design of a user model that can work regardless of the assessment units of users has in each chapter. Another student model is introduced to (Xu et al., 2002). It presents a fuzzy scientific logic in order to model the level of knowledge of the student. This is related to the content of the course, which in turn is shaped by learning activities and the possible history of interactions. All of these models (e.g. content and student) are defined by fuzzy logic. This system uses a database of student profiles to store the activities and interactions used to determine the student model. Taking into account the two models studied in this research, dynamic learning models were proposed for each student. Under the same rationale, the research of Jameson (1995) used fuzzy logic to design systems that allowed users or students to be modeled. It characterized each system within a common framework. There are also contributions to evaluation in this category. The smart system of Vrettaros et al. (2007) used fuzzy logic to assess and classify students' cognitive development. This assessment was performed in terms of performance, according to the structure of the observed learning outcome. An empirical approach is presented by Stathacopoulou et al. (1999) in the context of a smart teaching system for student assessment. The neuro-fuzzy model was developed as a quality student comparison model. This model was able to evaluate information about the student's knowledge and cognitive skills. With the aim of helping to determine the optimal educational approaches, Fazlollahtabar and Mahdavi (2009) used a neuro-fuzzy synergy offering possibilities for logic in the smart learning environments. The neuro-fuzzy process allowed knowledge to be coded for the teacher, using logic skills based on the students' learning mode.

3.2.1.3.3 Fuzzy Logic for Recommendation

Recommendation systems are the most classic application of fuzzy techniques. As mentioned above, this logic is the most appropriate for representing user preferences. In (Xu et al., 2002) used fuzzy logic to model the students and the content of an e-learning system. The authors also suggested the use of this logic for the dynamic adaptation of learning activities, including adaptive features in this educational system. Another approach is to model student groups. To this end, the study of Myszkorowski and Zakrzewska (2013) explored fuzzy numbers related to student characteristics. The similarity of the dominant characteristics of a student and the basic characteristics of the groups are taken into account for the design of an adapted sentence system for young students. Hsieh et al. (2012) proposed another recommender system that helps teachers decide which material is right for each student. Fuzzy inference mechanisms are used in this work. The aforementioned technique in conjunction with the preferences of the students, the prioritization of the procedures and the regular updates of the system created a fertile ground for the guidance of students by tutors.

The adaptive and intelligent educational system of Yu et al. (2001) also offers a new proposal system. It uses fuzzy matching rules to find the adequate educational materials that best suit the needs of each student. This recommender e-learning system can support students online and improved their experience.

3.2.1.3.4 Fuzzy Ontology

An example of the use of fuzzy ontologies appears in the research of Lau et al. (2009).

The authors proposed a novel mechanism for student groups using fuzzy ontology. For this purpose, the relationships between objects, classes and characteristics were described by fuzzy relationships. This fuzzy ontology automatically allowed the construction of conceptual groups. The data for the input came from the information that students gave through different pedagogical structures. The groups allowed teachers to analyze and monitor students' progress.

3.2.1.3.5 Fuzzy Logic for Clustering

Another aspect of educational data mining for e-learning systems is the grouping of learners based on their behavior. The goal concerning the learners is to be categorized into specific categories defined by their profiles. This approach supports decision making in e-learning systems. An example of this type of work appears in the work of Hogo (2010). The authors used different fuzzy grouping technologies to find students' categories and predict their preferences. Also, their experiments were designed using fuzzy grouping models. In analyzing their results, it should be noted that fuzzy approaches worked better than classic ones. Fuzzy adaptive resonance theory (Fuzzy ART) was used for this purpose. This model was able to learn and recognize categories in arbitrary sequences. Fuzzy ART is based on the theory of fuzzy sets in the neural network ART. The author adopted a group decision approach to evaluating educational websites. According to the theory of fuzzy logic, the method of fuzzy rules is used to determine the decision of the group. Based on an experimental approach, an educational site evaluator was developed. Such techniques are used to help students in their self-assessment. A two-phase fuzzy grouping technique and a learning algorithm were used to incorporate a pattern recognition algorithm. Fuzzy decision trees are also used in classification to improve e-learning systems. In (Damez et al., 2005), the authors used a fuzzy decision tree to classify students as beginners or experienced users automatically.

3.2.1.3.6 Concept-Based and Fuzzy Adaptive E-learning

Duhayyim and Newbury (2018) created an e-learning system which was intended to improve students' understanding and performance. It was based on three tools, a fuzzy logic system, a color-coded concept map and a ranked concept list.

Initially, there is the interface for tutors where they can connect and create courses, content categories, subcategories of courses and add educational material, which will be stored in the learning material database. They can also create a concept and identify its number, its weight and its name. They can also create tests, either before or after the course, assess the student's level of understanding of each subsection of the course, and store the results and test data in the database of the question bank. To achieve this, the values of conceptual errors were determined when teachers created the tests.

Furthermore, learning modalities have been used for the students to have a more personalized learning experience. Specifically, they can see the concept map of the lesson and have a better understanding of the its structure. They can start with a test to assess their knowledge level. The test is produced by a fuzzy logic system which then builds a color-coded concept map to show students their cognitive background and based on the test results, it creates a ranked concept list for the delivery of the learning material for each student, to better understand the course. Students should follow the sorted list to have the optimal learning experience of specific material. The material could be provided in various forms (text, audio and video). At the end of the lesson, students could take another test to create a new color-coded concept map that would show their new level of knowledge and progress.

To design and implement the tests, two input variables were defined, the concept weight and the concept error value as well as another variable, the concept impact. The tutor of the course was responsible for giving these two input values to the phases of the creation of the tests. The variable concept impact was used to give output values that will be sorted in the ranked concept list after each test. Tutors could create an unlimited number of multiple-choice questions. Each question was related to a domain to be taught, and aimed to determine the level of knowledge of students in each chapter. Students were allowed to choose only one answer for each question. Each question could belong to a cognitive category (form totally learnt to completely unknown). The error values of the answers were determined by the teacher.

After passing the tests, students received a color-coded concept map from the system which showed their cognitive level. They also received a color-coded concept map after the test, before the start of the learning process and at the end of it.

After the test, students received a sorted list of learning material. In order to achieve better results, they should attend the teaching material in the order in the ranked concept list. At the end of the learning process, they took a test to assess the level of knowledge they had at that time and to see their progress.

Finally, in terms of learning material, it could be in the form of multimedia, such as text, video or sound, and each student chose the way that suited him/her best. This material could only be added by the teacher of each lesson. However, the material that would be distributed to each student was determined based on the test.

3.2.1.3.7 The System of Fuzzy Logic

Fuzzy logic is used to assess students' level of knowledge, background, and identify appropriate educational material for each student. To build a system of fuzzy logic, firstly, the problem must be identified, the variables and the range of each should be defined and the fuzzy sets along with the fuzzy rules must be determined. Then, the fuzzy inference technique is applied. In order to complete the above, the following steps are followed:

- Definition of the problem and determination of language variables: In the pre-system the concept weight and the concept error value are taken as input variables, while the concept impact is taken as the output variable.
- Concept Weight: It is the first and most important variable as it determines the importance of each subsection of a course in order the optimal learning experience is achieved for each student. Its range is 0 to 1, with 1 being of high importance. The smaller this number becomes, the less important the subsection becomes too.
- Concept Error Value: The value of this variable can emerge from the results of the students in an assessment. It can have many language values to differentiate the level of knowledge of each student for each chapter.
- Concept Impact: It is the output variable and shows the degree to which the student has benefited from the learning process. It can have many values from low to high.
- Identification of fuzzy sets: A fuzzy set is a set of objects with fuzzy boundaries such as low, medium or high for the level of understanding of the chapter. To define a fuzzy set, a system can represent it as a function and then

distribute the elements of the set based on students' degree of participation. A representative example of a fuzzy set in a system is an unknown concept. The typical participation functions applied to fuzzy systems are either triangles or trapezoids.

- Constructing fuzzy rules: Once the input and output variables with their vague sets are determined, the system deals with fuzzy rules as in the figure, and the only one who can create fuzzy rules can be the tutor because s/he already knows how to solve the problem, using all language variables in their terms. Fuzzy rules are used because they consider the personal knowledge of each student as a parameter. A fuzzy rule is a selection structure (IF p is K, THEN q is L) where p and q are variables, and K and L are values defined by fuzzy sets.
- Fuzzy Inference: The steps followed are fuzzification of input variables, rule evaluation, aggregation of rule outputs and defuzzification.
  - Fuzzification: Initially the concept weight and concept error value inputs are received and it is determined to what extent these inputs belong to each relevant fuzzy set. At this stage, the participation rate of concept weight and concept error value is calculated. The concept weight and concept error value values are set by teachers when creating tests and modules. Teachers can give values between 0.0 and 1.0 that represent the concept weight. In addition, they give values between 0 and 100 to represent concept error value for each of the options during the tests. Once the entries are given, fuzzification occurs and they are clarified into fuzzy sets.
  - Rule Evaluation: The created fuzzy input values are applied to the fuzzy rules, from which some fuzzy values will emerge as outputs. Every rule of fuzzy conclusion could be defined by the students' prior knowledge. The output variables are defined as the fuzzy output of the variable.
  - Aggregation of the Rule Outputs: After the outputs from all the fuzzy rules are delivered, an aggregation of them is conducted to create a fuzzy set, which will be used to give a final output.
  - Defuzzification: It is the last stage in which the system takes the fuzzy set of outputs in order to give a final value that shows the student's progress.

Chapter 4:
Evaluation Methods of Intelligent Knowledge-Based Learning Technology Systems

As evaluation is an integral part of the life cycle of software, the research interest has been placed on proposing techniques and models for enhancing its quality. Evaluation can be seen as the recurrent process of data collection and analysis or classification in such a way that the final information can be used to determine whether the program effectively carries out the planned activities and whether it achieves the desired results[1].

Hence, for the evaluation of software, evaluation frameworks are used either for specific types of software (such as educational software) or in general. Therefore, a clear framework is needed to guide the monitoring and evaluation of software. Also, a framework should explain how the program should work and determine the components of the steps required to achieve the desired results. A framework increases the understanding of the program's objectives, determines the relationships between the key factors of the application and structures the internal and external elements that could affect the success of the program.

4.1   Evaluation

One approach to the definition of software evaluation is to consider it as the process that examines a program as a whole. It includes the collection and analysis of information about the activities, features and results of the program. Its purpose is to evaluate a program in order to improve its effectiveness and/or update planning decisions (Patton, 1987).

It is important to evaluate and periodically adjust the activities to ensure that they are as effective as possible. Evaluation supports the identification of points for improvement and ultimately assists the realization of the goals more effectively.

In view of the above, evaluation has three main goals. Firstly, it is to check the quality of the system, in terms of its weaknesses and strengths. Then, it is to check if the system results are the desired ones, depending on the preconceived goals. And finally, to be able to use the results properly, so that the system can be improved.

Usually, evaluation is considered superficially as the action of getting some results at the end of the program, in order to show that the program can work adequately. Nevertheless, evaluation can and should be used to improve the efficiency of a system.

Understanding how programs work – both in terms of effectiveness in delivering results as well as the impact of those results – is essential for informing each organization's decision-making strategy and resource allocation strategy. Without understanding what

---

[1] https://trust.guidestar.org/the-importance-of-evaluation

works well and what works poorly, it is not possible to systematically and consistently improve a program. Without rigorous evaluation, it is not possible to fully understand what works well.

Well-designed evaluations can help to confirm or revise the understanding of business needs around innovation and how to better meet those needs through targeted support. Over time, as databases are created, activities can be better designed to ensure maximum performance.

"Measurement is the first step that leads to control and ultimately to improvement. If you can't measure something, you can't understand it. If you don't understand it, you can't control it. If you can't control it, you can't improve it" as Harrington said[2].

4.1.1   Evaluation Framework

In view of the above, evaluations to monitor processes and results are considered imperative in order to determine how well a program achieves its goals. Determining an appropriate evaluation framework is a key component of evaluation design and is important for its planning. The best evaluation framework often depends on the type of program being evaluated but also on the resources available to conduct evaluation activities.

The frameworks used to evaluate programs include:

Process evaluation
Assess whether the program is implemented as originally planned, what services are provided, who receives these services, and the impression of the program among those interested.

Evaluation of results
Evaluate the extent to which a project has achieved its set goals and provides recommendations for future program improvements.

Antibody evaluation
Evaluate the impact of a program on participants and stakeholders, including the results and changes resulting from those results.

Performance monitoring
Evaluate the basic measurements in comparison to other data points in critical time points on a continuous basis throughout the implementation of the program. Service integration programs use the Plan–Do–Study–Act framework to incorporate new knowledge, make corrections and continuously improve programs (Taylor et al., 2014).

Cost-benefit assessment
Evaluates the relationship between project cost and results (or benefits). Policy makers, financial institutions and other stakeholders can use the evaluation findings to determine if an investment in the development and implementation of programs yields significant results of interest.

---

[2] https://rethinkyourmarketing.com/you-should-be-measuring-everything/

Investment Performance (Profit)
Often, the profit (ROI) for the program is calculated by preserving financial commitments.

4.1.2   Evaluation Frameworks for User Interfaces

Interactive systems are constantly evolving. This development leads to new challenges. One of these challenges is the quality of communication between interactive systems and people. This communication is essentially through the user interface. Evaluating the user interface is therefore significant to improve communication between a system and its users. Research on the evaluation of user interfaces is extensive (Krouska et al., 2017). Nevertheless, user interface evaluators still face difficulties.

Nowadays, interactive systems are used in all the research areas. Computers are transformed by calculating machines into indispensable tools that help users in various tasks. Then, their use could become more complicated and less convenient. Relevant user interfaces (UIs) evolve from console interfaces to handle inputs and outputs into complex interfaces, including further information and functions. This creates new challenges in promoting techniques for designing useful and reusable user interfaces (Ahlberg and Shneiderman, 1994).

Note that usability is defined by the ISO 9241-11 standard as follows: "The degree to which a product can be used by specific users to achieve specific goals with efficiency, effectiveness and satisfaction in a specific user context"[3]. A system is considered to be useful when it respects the utility factor of usefulness. Usefulness is defined by MacDonald Artwood (2014) as "the degree to which the functions of a system allow users to complete a set of tasks and meet specific objectives in a particular user context". The definition of usefulness faithfully reflects the characteristics of usability. This is because of the close relationship between usefulness and usability.

This challenge is amplified mainly by the application of fault-sensitive areas such as transportation, healthcare and the military. Thus, many recommendations, best practices, procedures and tools for evaluating and better designing UI have been proposed in the pertinent research literature (Park and Song, 2015). Despite the quality and quantity of these contributions, there is no consensus on a universal definition of the user interface evaluation. For example, Senach (1990) defines evaluation as a comparison between a reference project model and a project model that is observed in order to draw conclusions about UI evaluation. Other projects consider evaluation as the knowledge related to software ergonomics (i.e. ergonomic instructions and recommendations) validation, in combination with the interactive evaluation system, as is the case with (Charfi et al., 2013). In this case, the evaluation consists of ensuring that the UI complies with the recommendations and guidelines issued by the software ergonomics. Preece et al. (1994) define evaluation as the collection of utility data of a product by a specific group of users for a particular activity and within a particular environment.

The corresponding tools are many. They are mainly aimed at identifying aspects that can create utility problems (Park and Song, 2015) and minimize the risk of error. They also try to improve users' acceptance of interactive systems (Zhang et al., 1999). User interfaces are designed to improve and even optimize the efficiency and productivity of interactive systems (Zhang et al., 1999). Following, tools for user interface evaluation are presented.

---

[3] https://www.iso.org/obp/ui/#iso:std:iso:9241:-11:ed-2:v1:en

4.1.2.1   RITA (useR Interface evaluaTion frAmework)

Most tools available for User Interface Evaluation are based on a single technique. Each technique has its own evaluation features and incorporates different aspects of other techniques. It is interesting to use various techniques for evaluating interfaces. It is the main reason for the establishment of frameworks based on various evaluation techniques. Also, each evaluation tool is generally used to evaluate a specific type of UI, such as WIMP, Web or Mobile. Therefore, a tool that could be aligned to a multi-faceted evaluation would be very interesting. Important aspects of such an evaluation framework could be the following (Charfi et al., 2013):

- **General:** The framework is intended for the evaluation of various interaction systems. It supports the evaluation of WIMP, Web and Mobile interfaces.
- **Adjustable:** The framework is structured according to a modular architecture that can be configured to evaluate different UIs.
- **Flexible:** The framework follows ergonomic guidelines (EG) for interface evaluation. RITA encodes EG as external XML files. Therefore, the evaluator can add a new EG or modify the existing ones.
- **Multiple assessment techniques:** The tool is based on: (1) the evaluation of the static presentations of the UI, (2) ensuring user-system interaction, and (3) assessing the user's evaluated interface. In order to ensure that such an assessment is carried out, RITA takes advantage of three assessment techniques:
  - *Information delivery tool:* The tool collects real-time user activity information to analyze it and help the evaluator identify problems using the interface. This technique was chosen because it allows us to collect a lot of numerical data on the interaction that we can easily interpret and use for evaluation.
  - *Tool for controlling ergonomy quality:* The tool validates the compatibility of the interface using a set of ergonomic guidelines to detect design inconsistencies and ensure that the interface complies with these criteria. This technique allows the configuration of the selected ergonomic guidelines for evaluation in order to check the compatibility with the specific lines.
  - *Questionnaire:* It is used to assess the aspects that were impossible to be examined using the aforementioned techniques, such as clarity of error messages. The quality evaluation method allows the evaluator to ask the user mainly the reason and the way to solve a problem in the interface.

The interfaces are evaluated with RITA as soon as the system has already been implemented or in the case of a prototype, during the final design phase of the interactive system (test phase).

4.1.2.1.1 Functional Architecture of the RITA Framework

As mentioned above, RITA has a modular architecture. It includes four modules: *(1) Ergonomic Guidelines Manager, (2) Evaluation Data Capture Mode, (3) Evaluation Engine, (4) Evaluation Report Generator* (Charfi et al., 2013).

RITA inputs are provided in accordance with ergonomic guidelines, taking into account the interface source. RITA results include an evaluation report generated in the fourth module. The evaluation process has three phases: the first involves the preparation of data for evaluation. The second concerns the evaluation itself. The third involves creating the evaluation report.

- **Ergonomic Guidelines Manager**
  Since RITA does not have a strict code for ergonomic guidelines for evaluating interfaces, the evaluator must provide RITA with a set of ergonomic guidelines. This module allows the user to manage ergonomic guidelines and assists evaluators in managing an XML file database. An ergonomic guideline is defined by: (1) a numerical identifier, which is automatically assigned to the new guidelines, (2) a general description of the guideline, (3) related errors and recommendations in case of non-compliance with the guidelines (error and recommendations will be used for the report, by incorporating the identified errors and proposing improvement recommendations), (4) the relevant ergonomic criteria and the hypocrites to which they belong. the guidelines in this tool (Bastien), (5) the framework for using the guideline, where the framework is defined by the trinity <user, environment, platform> (Calvary et al., 2003), (6) a positive and a negative example for its representation the compatibility of the interface with the guideline, (7) the type of interface to which the guideline applies (WIMP, Web or Mobile) and (8) the author of the guideline and the source from which the guideline is derived.
- **Evaluation Data Capture Mode**
  This module is used to record different data for the evaluation process. RITA intends to examine (1) the static presentations of the user interface, (2) the quality of the user-interface interaction, and (3) the user's assessment of the evaluated interface. RITA then requires the recording of three categories of data (i.e. the presentation of the interface, user actions when interacting with the interface, and user satisfaction). This data is collected using three submodules:
  - *Generating questionnaire:* It is used to generate a database of questions. Each question is saved as an XML file. Closed-ended questions are usually used to make the process of analyzing users' answers easier, limiting their answers to one. The generator uses a set of questions to compose the questionnaire to evaluate the interface. The user then submits the answers which are processed by a third module (evaluation engine module–query analyzer). Please note that the evaluator has the absolute freedom to choose the appropriate questions for the questionnaire.
  - *Analysing Data for UI:* It extracts the values of the graphical control characteristics from the interface source. It can determine, using the provided submodule, the type of graphical control interface (e.g. button, text box, etc.) that will be used to extract the values of the characteristics. The source code of the interface is then specified. As an output we have the exported data stored in an XML file.
  - *Information delivery tool:* Its purpose is to detect and record low-level events (e.g. mouse cursor movement, user mouse clicks, and keyboard inputs). In addition, it helps the evaluator to relate these events to specific user tasks (i.e. to relate key actions to tasks). This classification breaks down the different interface events into two main categories: (1) Event interface of user, which includes the tasks used by the interface (for example, to open a window or read one error message), (2) Event of devices of interaction, including events created by interaction devices (such as right-

clicking a mouse or pressing a button on a keyboard). Interaction is formed through the event interface of user. The event interface of user is generated through the detected events of devices of interaction. Nevertheless, the information delivery tool provides the evaluator with some statistics such as the number of tasks performed by the user, the number of system tasks, and the success rate of tasks performed. Note that an event interface of user consists of one or more events of devices of interaction. Nevertheless, the information delivery tool provides the evaluator with some statistics such as the number of tasks performed by the user, the number of system tasks, and the success rate of tasks performed. Note that an event of devices of interaction consists of one or more events of devices of interaction. Nevertheless, the information delivery tool provides the evaluator with some statistics, such as the number of tasks performed by the user, the number of system tasks, and the success rate of tasks performed.

- **Evaluation Engine of Evaluation**

  The purpose of this module is to use four submodules to analyze the data generated by the Evaluation Data Capture Mode.

  ○ *Interaction Data Analyzer*

    This submodule is based on numerical data on user interface interaction. It provides some data, such as the total duration of work performed, the number of tasks performed per user and the execution of the sequence of events. These calculations are determined by decomposing tasks into basic facts collected by the electronic informant. The interaction data analyzer allows the evaluator to compare the sequence of actions performed by the user and the average sequence of events. The evaluation framework supports the frequency, sequence and links between tasks.

  ○ *Questionnaire Analyzer*

    This submodule analyzes user responses to questionnaires and provides numerical data on these answers to give the evaluator a comprehensive overview of the answers.

    For each question, the analyst calculates the number of users answering it and the analysis of various alternative answers.

  ○ *User Interface Inspector (UI Inspector)*

    The interface inspector is used to identify interface design problems based on the ergonomic guidelines set by the evaluator in the module of the first evaluation process. The entries for this submodule come from the XML file directory (modeling the guidelines in queries) and in an XML file with the values of the graphical controls of the interface (i.e. dimension, font and color of the controls). The interface inspector, then, performs the methods according to the comparative operators under consideration, in order to verify the coherence between the proposed values and the interface characteristics. The inspector provides two messages as outputs: errors and recommendations regarding disrespectful guidelines.

  ○ *Data Interpeter*

    Once the evaluator receives the evaluation data of the three submodules, s/he must compose the data to obtain a final evaluation result. Data synthesis involves grouping data according to user-supported tasks by the system. Three coefficients are linked for each task. These coefficients are numerical values between 0 and 1:

– The first factor (completion rate) corresponds to the proportion of users who have successfully completed the task (e.g. 0.5 means that half of the users were able to perform the task successfully).
– The second factor (positive feedback rate) corresponds to the ratio of positive responses from users to questionnaires related to this task, and
– The third factor (control call rate) includes the ratio of the graphical interface control used to perform this task according to the guideline set using the first module.

In the approved evaluation process, the electronic information rate is considered to be the highest. Interacting and analyzing interaction data is the most reliable evaluation technique of the three techniques used. It is based on quantitative numerical data. In addition, it does not require subjective judgments from the evaluator. The results of the ergonomic quality inspection and the questionnaire complete the results of the electronic informant.

Note that the correlation between different types of data is created by aligning different work data per job. A task can be performed through many different screens. The correspondence between the controls and the tasks is determined through the list of required controls for each task. The correlation between work and question is determined manually by the evaluator.

- **Evaluation Report Generator**
This module compiles the evaluation report in a comprehensible and legible form. The report mainly includes identified design problems, recommendations for improving the interface and an overview of the evaluation process. The report can be exported in three different formats: PDF, HTML and TXT.

4.1.2.1.2 Proposed Evaluation Process
The user interface evaluation process using the RITA framework requires the participation of several stakeholders: (1) the evaluator (to manage and assist in the evaluation process), (2) an expert on human factors (to select and define ergonomic guidelines), (3) of the users (to participate in the interaction sessions), and (4) of the designer (to enter code into the system being evaluated so as to allow the electronic informant to collect data on the interaction).

- **Pre-evaluation phase:** In this phase, the evaluator begins with: (1) the definition of the evaluation objectives, (2) the determination of the scope of use of the evaluated system, (3) the determination of a list of ergonomic guidelines followed during the control of compliance with the interface, (4) setting a list of questions to ask users, (5) creating a questionnaire, (6) designing a scenario for session interaction, (7) preparing the material needed for evaluation, and (8) conducting the interaction session with the users.
- **Evaluation phase:** This phase involves extracting the data needed to identify the utility and utility problems of the interface. The data collected is: graphical interface control features, user responses and interaction data. The collected data is then processed and combined to help the evaluator evaluate the interface.

- **Phase after evaluation:** An evaluation report is first produced. The evaluation report includes the result of the evaluation: (1) a list of design problems identified in the evaluated interface, (2) a list of suggestions and recommendations for improving the interface, and (3) a report on the progress of the evaluation process. It covers the problems that arose during this process.

  Once the report is created, the designer applies the various suggestions and recommendations to improve the interface being evaluated. Depending on the results of the evaluation, and the limitations of the project (time and cost), the evaluator may proceed with a re-evaluation.

In summary, the RITA evaluation framework includes three main phases. The second and third phases are supported by the evaluation framework (note that with the exception of the different data evaluation compositions, these two phases are created automatically).

4.1.3   Evaluation Frames for Educational Systems

There are many factors that can complicate the process of evaluating interactive products by children but also it is often common to face difficulties in evaluating software by adults, meaning that pertinent studies often need to be planned with a little more care.

Since Child-Computer Interaction (CCI) is a relatively new field, there are few experts in CCI around the world, which means that most researchers who work to evaluate software with children are experts mainly in user utility and experience or children's education or psychology or related disciplines. It can be difficult for newcomers to the field to know all the necessary issues to consider. As any group of users, children also have their own needs and requirements that designers and evaluators must take into account, and for newcomers who are not used to working with children, this familiarity can be a complicated activity.

Evaluators for adults will, of course, have greater access to adult participants than to children. Evaluating with children usually means the involvement of specific stakeholders. Setting up a busy school schedule can also be a negative factor for conducting the evaluation, and combining this with the need to adapt to a daily school day with the need to understand children's little attention often leads to very primitive research studies. Children also need some other motivation or reward to participate, such as having fun in their studies, and in order to attend a school, they may want to see a visible and direct benefit.

In addition to these practical difficulties, researchers have proposed different methods for evaluating software by children, and many established evaluation methods may not be appropriate. Many imperfections have been identified using well-known research methods (e.g. Horton and Read, 2008, Borgers and Hox, 2001), due to problems such as child misunderstanding or just a different understanding of the world. Observation methods are often used, but require trained observers and are always at risk of prejudice. These difficulties have led to more and more to the creation of new methods to be designed or adapted specifically for children. The important point to note is that there are many methods, many of which have specific problems when used with children and which may have advantages or disadvantages depending on the purpose of the study. As the field of CCI evolves, new or modified evaluation methods often appear. Due to this fact, it can be very difficult to choose the right method for the most effective evaluation of software for children. The following are some relevant evaluation frameworks for educational systems.

4.1.3.1 Kirkpatrick's Four-Level Evaluation Framework

In 1954, Kirkpatrick created a four-level model, which is particularly helpful in effectively evaluating a system (Kirkpatrick, 1979). It is a multilevel model in which the highest level can only be achieved if the lowest levels are satisfactory. The model is briefly explained, as follows:

Level 1: Reaction
To what extent do user in a learning program react? (Did they enjoy the training? Did they complete it?)

Level 2: Learning
To what extent do users acquire the expected knowledge, skills and attitudes that emerge after using the educational system. (Did they pass the assessment? What skills and knowledge did they acquire?)

Level 3: Behavior or Transfer
To what extent do users apply what they have learned from the educational software? (Do they work better? Which of the following did they apply?)

Level 4: Results
To what extent are the desired goals achieved as a result of the educational software? In short, the impact that the education system has on the performance of the participants. (Did the company's measurements improve? Was the result profitable?)

Kirkpatrick based his model on four questions about educational software:

1. Did they like it?
2. Did they find out?
3. Will they use it?
4. Will anything change?

These four levels represent the basis of the Kirkpatrick model. But the key is to use the model in the right way, which means starting at level 4 and going upside down.

4.1.3.1.1 The Kirkpatrick Model Pyramid

Efficiency of Kirkpatrick Model
There are definitely strengths and weaknesses in all relevant models. But indeed, it is not so important the model which is used that matters, but the way it is used.

In most cases, the Kirkpatrick Model works adequately. It is important to start applying it right, having a clear idea of the result to be achieved and then to work upside down (backwards) on how to achieve it.

Reaction
This level shows how the stakeholders in education react. Did they like it? Do they find it useful? Did they like the educational process, the design and the tutor? In this level, it is not discovered the fulfilment of the learning goals as well as the learning outcomes. This is what the next levels do. However, it gives an idea of how they perceived it and

how the user experience can be improved.

This can be achieved by sharing questionnaires after the learning process, asking participants to state how they found the lesson. Gathering the answers, significant observations can be provoked, such as if they had difficulty with the instructions, if they found the narration annoying, etc. Very useful information can emerge and the questionnaire is quite easy to be made.

Learning

The goal of learning that participants have is to learn. However, there are several issues, such as: Did the participants really learn from the material? How much has their knowledge increased?

A good way to evaluate this is with two tests – one at the beginning and one at the end of the lesson. By asking questions on the same topic, it can be seen if participants answer more questions correctly after learning. If they answer correctly, it means that they have learned. If not, then something is probably wrong with the material in our lesson.

This can be a useful assessment method, as it can give us specific information. If all participants are wrong in answering questions about a particular topic, then we need to look again at how this topic is taught. What is not clear for students? How can we better present it so that participants can understand the lesson?

Another way to evaluate this is with the use of a questionnaire after the lesson. But in addition to the basic questions of level 1, students can asked to declare what they learned in this lesson. In some cases, this may be more accurate than a test. Asking participants to describe themselves in their own words can show how much they really understand.

Behavior

Many people have been in similar classes where they learn about a specific topic and return in their everyday life showing poor possibility to use the knowledge they acquired. That is probably not an issue arisen by the lack of knowledge. People probably know the right process. The problem is that knowledge has not been applied. The third level of the Kirkpatrick model refers to: Do participants use what they have learned?

This is often something that need to be evaluated shortly after the interaction with the course. The best way to achieve this is using 360-degree feedback. This feedback derives from the participants, their colleagues and their supervisors. If the learning has the desired result, this will be perceived by all the stakeholders.

Sometimes feedback can indicate that no change has been made. In these cases, it is important to ask the participants to detail on their point of view. Behavior can only change if the conditions for it are favorable. Will the teacher let the participants apply their knowledge? Is there any tool that has not been implemented? Does the learner have the desire or motivation to apply what s/he has learned? What can be done about these cases?

The latest assessment level of the Kirkpatrick model examines whether the learning has a positive effect on the business.

This is based on the goals set before the process of education. Important queries can be: What changes do teachers want? How do they define success? In a different case, the expected results cannot be analyzed.

The way to evaluate this will be determined by the expected. Typically, this involves data analysis. When evaluating the impact of education, it is important to know all the aforementioned levels. For example, if the behavior of a student has not changed, it is crucial to check the previous states to understand why the participants really learn what they needed to learn. And if not, it is important to explore if it was because of a confusing learning design that could not assist students. That is why it is significant to organize the evaluation of the educational system so that it covers all the four levels. In this way, an overview of the effectivity of the learning process can be available as well as improvement steps can be appeared.

4.1.3.2 The CIAO Evaluation Framework

Another model for the assessment of learning technologies is the CIAO (Jones, 1999). This framework was developed to evaluate the learning applications but also became the basis for the evaluation of other external tools.

The framework describes three dimensions of evaluation: content, interactions, and attitudes and outcomes. Following, more information of each dimension is given.

- The content is defined as the detailed analysis of the software-based logic, as well as the goals that should have been achieved after its use.
- The interactions refer to the students' interactions with the computer, but also to each other so that they understand that this also helps the learning process.
- The outcomes refer to the analysis of the changes observed in the students after their interaction with the learning technology system.

These are shown in the table below.

Table 1. The CIAO framework (Jones et al., 1999)

	Content	**Interactions**	**Attitudes and outcomes**
Logic-thinking	Objectives and content of use	The data from the students' interactions with the software that allows the analysis of the process	It is important to try to evaluate the learning outcomes but also to consider emotional outcomes, e.g. perceptions and attitudes
Data	The goals of the designer and the lesson groups, policy documents and records of the meetings	Records (practical) of students' interactions. Student work products. Student diaries Online logs	Learning measurements Changes in students' behavior and perception
Methods	Interview with the developers and member of the course team Analysis of policy documents	Observation Calendar Audiovisual recordings and computer recordings	Interviews Questionnaires Test

The following are the reasons for the emphasis on the two dimensions mainly, the content and the interactions and the consequences of this emphasis on the evaluation of digital systems.

Content

The content includes the number of aspects of the course such as the location as well as the participants, the way a particular application is used, and the designer's goal for the digital learning system, as it is very important in the evaluation. The framework includes various areas including the rationale of the presentation of technology, the content of the course (i.e., how it is related to other parts of the course), the content of the use and to what extent and how human teaching is supported.

The collection of this data is done through interviews. So, the system designers to the members of the course will be interviewed in order to determine the goal and logic of the system.

Interactions

The aim of the study and analysis of students' interactions is to better understand the learning process. Thus, students are monitored while using the system and their interactions are recorded in order to collect data for further analysis. Also, all the actions performed by the students during the use of the system are collected.

Results

In addition to the above, the knowledge gained after using the software is very important as both teachers and students need to know the results of teaching and learning respectively. Thus, it is analyzed what students are expected to be able to do after the course and what they have achieved. As such, these results help to see if the software is really effective.

Aim of the CIAO Evaluation Framework

The goal of CIAO is to provide a variety of methods for specific evaluations than to propose a specific approach. It focuses on education, at least emphasizing both on the process and the results, which in turn leads to the emphasis on observation so that empirical data can be collected. The choice of methods can best be applied to a wide range of contents. Several evaluation approaches also emphasize the need for a variety of tools and the problems of controlled studies. However, there is no detailed guidance on how to apply specific methods for the content that is not commonly used. This cannot be considered as problematic; qualitative evaluation will include understanding the scope, suitability and applicability of the methods, as with any research skill, evaluation is not a special case. It does mean, however, that it will be important for the evaluator to understand learning technologies and to appreciate the benefits that specific technologies can offer. Using user-centered assessment methods will help students make better use of the technologies offered.

4.1.3.3   ROI Methodology (Five ROI Framework)

The ROI methodology consists of five key elements that work together to complete the evaluation puzzle. These elements are linked in order to create a complete evaluation system.

The system begins with the five-level ROI framework, developed in the 1970 by Jack Philips[4]. It is based on the model of Kirkpatrick. In this model, there is the fifth level of ROI which transformed the model into operational with practical tools. This framework is used to categorize the results of all types of programs and tasks.

---

[4]   https://roiinstitutecanada.com/wp-content/uploads/2014/02/Application-Guide.pdf

Level 1: Reaction and Scheduled Energy data represent the reactions of the program and the planned actions of the participants. Reactions may include views on structure, ease of use, comfort and convenience. This category should include data that reflects the value of the program's content, including relevance, amount of new information, and willingness of participants to recommend the program to others.

Level 2: The Learning Data represent to what extent participants have acquired new knowledge about their strengths, development areas, and skills needed to be successful. This category also includes the level of self-confidence of the participants as they plan to apply the new knowledge and skills in their work.

Level 3: Implementation and Execution Data determine to what extent professionals apply their new knowledge and skills from the learning program. This category of data also includes data describing the obstacles that may cause difficulties in using the learning program as well as any supporting elements in the knowledge transfer and skills process.

Level 4: Several data is collected and analyzed to determine the extent to which the application of the acquired knowledge and skills has a positive effect on the basic measures that are to be improved as a result of the learning experience. Measures include errors, rejections, new accounts, complaints, sales, time, life cycle, commitment to study and compliance. By stating the data at this level, a step is always taken to separate the effect of the program on these measures.

Level 5: Profit compares the monetary benefits of the impact (as they are converted into monetary value) with the full cost of the program. The cost of the program plays an important role and should be compared to the disposal of the program to learning organizations and/or universities. If the monetary value of the sales improvement exceeds the cost, the calculation is a positive return on investment (ROI).

Each evaluation level answers key questions about the success of the program, as follows.

Table 2.

Evaluation level	Key questions
Level 1: **Reactions and** **scheduled actions**	• Was the lesson about work and role? • Was the lesson important for the work and success of the participants? • Did it give new information to the participants? • Will they use what they have learned? • Would they recommend the program or process to others? • Does the duration or structure of the course need to be improved?
Level 2: **Learning**	• Did the participants acquire the knowledge and skills identified at the beginning of the course? • Do participants know how to apply what they have learned? • Do they feel confident in applying what they have learned?
Level 3: **Application and** **execution**	• How effectively do they apply what they have learned? • How often do they apply what they have learned? • Are they successful in applying what they have learned? • If they apply what they have learned, what is it that supports them? • If they don't apply what they've learned, why not?
Level 4: **Business copy**	• If the application is successful, what impact does this have on the business? • To what extent does the application of knowledge and skills improve the measures of the business that the program aimed to improve? • How has the program affected sales, productivity, operating costs, life cycle, errors, rejection, work commitment and other measures? • How do we know that the curriculum was the one that improved these measures?
Level 5: **ROI**	• Are the financial benefits of improving business impact measures above the cost of a technology-based learning program?

Evaluation Framework and Key Questions

By categorizing assessment data based on the levels, a clear and understandable framework is provided for the management of the design and objectives of learning technologies as well as for the management of the data collection process. More importantly, these five levels present the data in a way that makes it easy for people to understand the results reported for the program. While each level of evaluation provides important, autonomous data, when reported together, the five-level ROI framework presents data that shows the actual success or failure of the program. As a consequence, they positively affect the basic measures of the business. When these measures are converted into monetary value and compared to the total cost, then the profit (ROI) is calculated. Along with ROI and the other four categories of data, intangible interests are also mentioned. These are presented in level 4 and are not converted into monetary value.

4.1.3.4   The Five Levels of Kaufman Evaluation

Kaufman's five evaluation levels[5] are a reaction and development of Kirkpatrick's four-level model. While Kirkpatrick's model divides evaluation by type of influence (impact), especially for the learner, Kaufman's model evaluates the effect on different groups.

An interpretation of Kaufman's levels is summarized in the following table, which includes the corresponding Kirkpatrick levels.

---

[5]   https://kodosurvey.com/blog/kaufmans-model-learning-evaluation-key-concepts-and-tutorial

Table 3.

Kaufman	Kirkpatrick	Explanation
Entrance	1a	*Availability of resources and quality* These are educational materials, digital resources, etc., used to support the learning process.
Procedure	1b	*Efficiency and effectiveness of the process* This is the actual meaning of burning up of bad psychic imprints.
Micro	2 and 3	*Remuneration of individuals and small groups* This is the result for the "micro-level customer" (usually the student). Did the student acquire the learning?
Macro	4	*Benefits of the organization* This is the result for the "macro-level customer" for the organization and includes evaluation of performance improvement and cost analysis and cost consequences.
Mega	None	*Social contributions* This is the result for the "high level" stakeholder.

Entry and Procedure

The Kaufman's most practical and useful suggestion is to divide Kirkpatrick's level one into an entry and a process. In a world that allows easy and fast access to websites, the availability and quality of Internet-based resources are becoming increasingly important evaluation factors. Different types of questions need to be asked when assessing the availability of resources in relation to delivery, so it helps to think about them separately. The focus on resource availability may seem similar to Kirkpatrick's proposed 0-level (introduction) but this is happening socially by evaluating any informal learning.

Kaufman also replaces Kirkpatrick's measure of learner satisfaction with learning experience, directly examining the learning and delivery resources themselves. It is useful to note that Kaufman acknowledges that while the input from learners is important when evaluating this data, it is not the only source of data.

Micro-Level Assessment

Grouping levels 2 and 3 of Kirkpatrick is less useful, as performance can and should be evaluated separately. Good assessment and simulation can record data about learning. The performance can then be monitored to assess whether the learning has been applied correctly in the workplace.

Having this evaluation data is important because it will determine the best way to resolve any issue. For example, the solutions for students who have not been able to apply what they have learned are different from the solutions of those who have not been able to learn them from the beginning.

Six Levels

In the final presentation of the five assessment levels, Kaufman tries to reflect Kirkpatrick's levels, possibly to serve those who know Kirkpatrick. As a result, Kaufman maintains entry and the process together as Levels 1a and 1b of his model. At the same time, Kirkpatrick's Levels 2 and 3 are kept separate but are called "Micro-Level".

Kaufman's six levels include:

1. Entry
2. Procedure
3. Acquisition
4. Application
5. Organization Results
6. Social Consequences/Consequences for the customer

Mega-Level Assessment

The additional requirement to evaluate social consequences makes the Kaufman model less practical than Kirkpatrick's. Some unsubstantiated evidence about the social impact can be gathered, but obtaining data at such a high level is often not possible. While it is helpful to look at the impact of learning on customers and society in some cases, evaluation can often be included in the goal that learning is expected to achieve.

For example, if learning is expected to improve skills, more students will benefit because they use a very good prototype. It is not necessarily helpful to assess that the student benefits separately from achieving the learning goal. Even if the goal is improving student's satisfaction, it does not have to be seen as a separate level.

Kirkpatrick's original model was designed for formal education. Kaufman's model is almost equally limited, seeking to be useful in any kind of learning (including informal learning).

In practice, the Kirkpatrick's model can be also used in environments other than formal education. While the model was designed with formal education in mind, most professionals are realistic enough to interpret the model for their own specific contexts.

4.1.3.5   Anderson's Learning Model

The learning value model (Anderson's Value of Learning) was published by the Chartered Institute of Personnel and Development and was based on research from the United Kingdom University of Portsmouth in 2006[6]. It aims to address two challenges:

- **The challenge of evaluation:** This is very important since many educational organizations report that they are struggling to make a good assessment.
- **The challenge:** Leaders of educational organizations often require evidence that demonstrates the value of learning and tutoring as well as the efficient use of resources.

This model is cyclic and intended to be applied at the body level and not in specific learning interventions.

Step 1: Identify the current adjustment with the strategic priorities

This stage assesses how closely the organization's learning is tailored to your its strategic priorities. To what extent does your learning strategy support this focus? Achieving high adaptation requires the knowledge of the organization's strategic priorities and to develop a learning strategy that supports those priorities.

---

[6]   http://hdl.voced.edu.au/10707/106984

Stage 2: Use a series of methods to evaluate and evaluate the contribution of the course.

This stage assesses the contribution of learning through a series of measures. The model does not specify exactly these measures, but describes four areas of evaluation that need to be covered.

- **Learning operation measures**
  How effective and efficient is the learning process within the educational organization? This includes the learning team and any stakeholder supporting education in the organization.
- **Measures to meet expectations**
  To what extent have the expectations of specific learning programs and interventions been met?
- **Profit measures**
  How much did the specific learning programs and interventions cost and how does is this compared to the revenue generated and/or the savings spent?
- **Comparative evaluation and power measures**
  How are learning processes and performance compared to internal or external standards? This assessment should be monitored continuously in order the progress is identified.

Stage 3: Determine the most relevant approaches for your body.

The model recognizes that organisations differ, and therefore the measures described in the second stage will be more or less significant depending on the specific needs of an organisation. For example, some organizations already recognize that learning is their cornerstone and want to ensure that they invest in the right initiatives. Similarly, some groups focus on short-term learning benefits, while others focus more on long-term benefits.

As such, it is important to choose a mix of metrics that best suits the needs of the organization.

Table 4. The value model of Anderson's learning

	The confidence of senior executives in the contribution of learning	The organization requires measurements of learning values
Emphasis on short-term benefits	Learning operation measures	Profit measures
Emphasis on long-term benefits	Measures to meet expectations	Comparative evaluation and power measures

Focus on learning strategy

Focusing the learning value model on learning strategy and adapting to the organization's strategic priorities is extremely helpful. For example, an organization may implement Kirkpatrick's model to evaluate a learning program designed to increase its productivity. The evaluation shows that the program is successful if productivity increases.

Restrictions

The Anderson's Value of Learning model is high-level and flexible, making it less useful in offering practical guidance on specific evaluations. For example, the model encourages organizations to evaluate the effectiveness and efficiency of learning as a whole, but provides minimal guidance on how to measure effectiveness or efficiency.

In practice, this model must be combined with other models, such as the Kirkpatrick's model, in order to achieve the detail of individual learning initiatives to give an overall picture of the effectiveness of learning in the body.

4.1.3.6 Brinkerhoff's Success Case Method

Educational organizations' effort is to become more efficient and competitive. stakeholders at all levels are increasingly using new technologies in all areas of their work. The Success Case Model (SCM) is designed to address and exploit this reality.

SCM is a carefully balanced mix of storytelling with more modern methods and principles of rigorous evaluation and research. SCM is also practical. It is important to use well-founded research principles to search for the right stories to tell and support them with substantiated evidence.

The Main Questions of SCM

An SCM study can be used to get answers to four key questions:
- What is the description of the environment?
- What results does the program seek to generate?
- What is the value of the results?
- How could the initiative be improved?

The SC research addressed to these questions and can range from the simplest to the most complex. At the simplest part of the spectrum, an SC survey can only be used to discover and illustrate the ways for which a new innovation is being used or to help determine if advancements are identified as a result of a new program or change. In a more complex part, an SC study can indicate the characteristics of people, the organizational units, the use of novel tools and methods, and the success they have. At the even more complex part of the spectrum, an SC study can provide estimates for profits and help to make decisions about how much the program is estimated to offer advancements of the level of performance.

Following, four key questions and some explanations are shown to depict the scope of the research:

1. *What is the description of the environment?* This basic question has a number of applications. At the most fundamental end of the complexity spectrum, a quick SC study can be used simply to illustrate the types factors affecting a new initiative. Here are some more specific questions that SC studies can be used to answer:
   ◦ Who uses the novel methods and who does not?
   ◦ Which parts of the new innovations are used and which are not?
   ◦ How widespread is the use?
   ◦ Which groups or subgroups make the least, or most, use of new techniques?
   ◦ When are the methods used?

2. *What results does the program seek to generate?* Almost all SC studies can gather data on the most results produced by a different initiative, and can provide rich illustrations of these results. If there are no positive results for the program at all, the SC method will quickly discover it.

The SC study can be used to detect desired or undesirable results. It is very easy to combine estimates of results with estimates of how many people make different uses of a program.

3. *What is the value of the results?* In many cases, and when it is desirable to do so, it is possible to extend the SC method to assess the economic value of the successful results achieved. When the monetary values of the results are estimated, they can then be compared with the costs of the program, and an estimate of the profit or return on profit can be made.

   These value and cost estimates are, of course, only as good as the cost and value assumptions on which they are based. Such assessments are possibly incomplete and assumptions are always open to questions and discussions. For these reasons, making statements about the value and return of costs are avoided unless those statements are clearly and unquestionably justifiable.

   Sometimes, it is helpful to combine estimates of monetary value of results with estimates of the range and distribution of the use of new methods and tools. If a new proposal seems to be producing good results, but only for a small portion of the participants, then it is likely that there will be a greater value that still needs to be collected from the program.

4. *How could the initiative be improved?* This SC question expands the research to evaluate these success factors of the program so that additional program users can increase their success and come closer to the highest levels of success achieved by the most successful. users. Often, it is not only the tools or methods of the program that make the biggest difference in success, but specific environmental factors used to make innovation feasible. In an educational program, for example, one part of the body can use an extra motivation and this motivation combined with the learning achieves unparalleled results.

Use the Success Case approach
The SC method has a variety of useful uses. New benefits have emerged and readers who use the method will certainly experience even more. Below the most common uses of the SC method are discussed.

- *It quickly and easily discovers what works and what does not with the new changes and suggestions.* Each new change proposal is highly predictable on the one hand: it will almost never be fully complete, nor will it be a major failure. With a new proposal that mostly has good results, the challenge is to detect the successful ways for better results. With a suggestion that mostly does not work, the trick is to avoid utilizing misconceptions in the approach. These few elements of the program that are worth saving must be recognized and used for better performance.

- *It explains the results and achievements in a way that is interesting and exciting.* Even when a program works well, there will always be several stakeholders who question its effectiveness and want to see evidence that it makes a difference. The SC method produces interesting illustrations as real user stories are explored.

- *It provides models and examples to motivate and guide others.* Similarly, the SC method helps young users of a proposal to discover the ways in which others have applied tools and methods to serve as a guide and inspiration for their own practice. The SC method learners with a clear and specific picture of how exactly some of their colleagues started using something and made it work.

- *It recognizes requirements quickly and practically, to evaluate the success or failure of a new proposal.* At some point, a new program or change is subject to re-examination. The SC method is a powerful and convincing evaluation approach that provides unquestionable evidence, which will be able to figure out how well a program works and what kind of valuable results it produces.

How the SC Method Works

An SC study has a very simple two-part structure. The first part of the study involves identifying possible success cases, involving stakeholders who were obviously most successful in using a new change or method. The first step is often achieved with research. Although research is often used, it is not always necessary. It may be possible to identify potential cases of success by reviewing user files and reports and accessing data. One survey can be used more often because it provides the added benefit of having results to obtain quantitative estimates of the percentages of people who report using some new method or innovation. Also, when careful sampling methods are used, then estimates of the probability of the nature and extent of success can also be determined.

Almost always, an SC study also examines cases of failure. Exploring the reasons for lack of success can be very enlightening and helpful. Comparisons between groups are particularly useful.

4.1.3.7   The Four-Dimensional Framework (FDF)

The extensive report of Second Life (SL) – a social virtual world – helped to emphasize the use of virtual worlds to support a variety of human activities and interactions, presenting a variety of new opportunities and challenges to enrich the way with which people learn (e.g. Prasolova-Førland and Divitini, 2003), as well as the way they work and play. In this way, SL, like other virtual world applications, has enabled users and students, teachers and learners, policy makers and decision makers to easily collaborate in 3D environments regardless of real distance. time. The basis of these experiences is the presence of the learner or user as an "avatar" in the virtual space. This avatar represents the user's visualization in the virtual space and facilitates a greater sense of control within the virtual environments, allowing users to more easily participate in real-time experiences (Gazzard, 2009).

The general use of virtual environments in recent years has been greatly facilitated through Internet-based technologies and applications, as well as increasing the bandwidth and capabilities of graphics computers. These improvements allow for a range of learning and educational options, including document and file sharing, meeting and event organization, networking and virtual seminars, lectures and conferences, research experiments, and international meetings (e.g. De Freitas, 2010). Such applications have even greater capabilities for integrating different technologies, supporting social software applications (e.g. Facebook, Flickr and Wikipedia), presenting materials and content of e-learning and offering students games and rich social interactions. In addition, customized electronic virtual platforms have been developed, mainly from universities and research institutes, mainly for educational and learning purposes (e.g. Liarokapis al., 2004). These are more experimental prototypes and usually use specialized hardware devices such as advanced visualization (screens mounted on the head, stereoscopic screens), interaction (3D mouse, orientation and position sensors) as well as tactile (gloves). However, usually the costs associated with these types of configurations remain very high, compared to the alternatives listed above.

This flexibility in use along with the possible global user attraction led to the sudden and widespread development of virtual world applications. While not all of these virtual worlds are applicable to learning and many are aimed at young children (e.g. Club Penguin[7]), the scope is not only about the potential use for education and training but also the actual use by users. Both the widespread appearance and the possibility of applying these virtual learning spaces have aroused great interest in instructors to learn more about how they can be better used in the classroom and seminars.

However, the range of virtual world applications and their relatively rapid appearance have made this space a challenge for researchers and teachers (Hendaoui, Limayem and Thompson, 2008). The area is fragmented due to the nature of its interdisciplinary appearance and the literature is scattered around a number of scientific disciplines.

By supporting this interdisciplinary approach in the field of serious games and virtual worlds, the authors in previous works tried to redefine ideas about learning, especially away from the more traditional approaches and the concept of learning more focused on experience and exploration (Tan et al., 2017). To further understand this, the role of multimodal interfaces (e.g. 3D interfaces) and perceptual modeling (knowledge-based approaches) should be considered, as our interactions with the environment and our social interactions with others create an approach of constructing learning experiences as a series of educational steps process instead of relying on data retrieval strategies (De Freitas et al., 2010). This approach reorganizes the way people produce and develop learning activities, with a greater emphasis on student control, greater commitment, content created by students, and communities supported by peers, which together can increase learning profits. More specifically, a former study tested the "Four-Dimensional Framework (FDF)" developed in previous studies (De Freitas et al., 2010). in content created by students and in communities supported by peers, which together can increase learning profits.

Most bibliographic evaluation frameworks for exploring uses and designing learning activities in virtual worlds are generally focused on education (e.g. Fu et al., 2008). Therefore, many evaluation studies adopted an inductive methodology, which requires researchers to construct theories and explanations based on observations made using educational research approaches, including the use of data and observations (De Freitas et al., 2010).

In addition to the inductive method, the study (De Freitas et al., 2010) combined the use of the "four-dimensional framework" to provide a more structured approach to the composition and analysis of research findings. The framework emerged from user studies with teachers and learners around game selection and use based on play. However, it has been used to support the game design and development process (De Freitas et al., 2010). The framework suggests four dimensions: the student, the pedagogical models used, the representation used and the context in which learning takes place.

The first dimension includes a process of profiling and modeling the learner and his/her requirements. This profile ensures a close correspondence between the learning activities and the required results. Emphasis on the learner can in turn emphasizes the

---

[7] https://cprewritten.net/

importance of the interaction between the learner and his environment. For example, more normal interactions may provide less gaps in learning transfer. Information and communication technology (ICT) skills can affect the way a student interacts with his/ her experience and abilities to devote him/herself to activities in the first place.

The second dimension analyzes the pedagogical perspective of learning activities and includes an examination of the types of learning and teaching models adopted in parallel with the methods of supporting learning processes. This may include the use of correlational models based on project-based learning approaches and according to learning methodology and constructive learning models that involve the use of existing knowledge by the learner. "Social" learning models involve more socially shaped approaches to learning (e.g. Wenger's practice community practice model, 1998). The particular choice of learning theories can predict the types of learning outcomes that arise. For example, experiences based on project-based analysis and the construction of learning work lead to specialized outputs and although effectiveness may be limited to learning environments based more on education. Also, some forms may more easily enhance those approaches.

The third dimension describes the representation itself, how the interactive learning experience should take place, what levels of engagement are required, and how beneficial the experience is. The representational dimension includes "narration" or the application of experience and can affect levels of engagement and motivation.

The final dimension of the framework can affect where learning takes place, for example, in school or informal settings. It can also affect the disciplinary framework, for example, which topic is being studied and whether the learning is conceptual or applied. The environment may also include the support resources used for learning. The interactions between the trainee and his/her environment are particularly important as the trainee can be present in both physical and virtual space at the same time. These hybrid spaces are relatively unexplored in terms of research, but they can allow different approaches to learning beyond those described here.

Each dimension has dependencies on the others. However, together, the four dimensions provide a conceptual framework for exploring learning in a virtual environment and, in our view, have an impact on the design of learning as a whole, especially when applied to virtual learning environments.

4.1.3.8 *The SECAL Evaluation Framework*

The SECAL (Situated Evaluation of Computer-Assisted Learning) assessment framework (Gunn, 1997) is based on the assumption that experimental evaluations fail to determine which individual or combined factors support learning. It is argued that evaluations should be designed to take these factors into account, rather than trying to balance or ignore them. "Assessment in the context" examines the first results of the use of technology in CAL. Adequate integration of learning technologies into the lessons is important. The "framework assessment" examines the factors that are indirectly related to the learning technology program or the learning environment. Factors related to institutional support levels for acquiring, developing and using learning technologies are incorporated into this latter category. As a result, authenticity is a prerequisite for the framework. There is also a dynamic aspect of SECAL that supports the establishment and implementation of beneficial changes in learning environments.

The application of this framework implies that authenticity in study design must be an integral factor. Therefore, evaluation is limited in scope and frequency by the number of target users and the opportunities available to evaluate the results of learning technologies as a fully integrated part of the course. Although these limitations may seem very restrictive, the integrated and theoretically supported SECAL framework is successfully applied in very different conditions and produces relative and substantial results. The experimental goals of generalized results and the production of theory are not excluded, they just take more time to achieve.

In this framework, it is simple to adjust the frame by weighing each item according to its relevance in a particular case.

A brief description of the structure and implementation of an evaluation framework designed to meet the current requirements of CAL researchers can be summarized in four points:

- create a detailed search of the evaluation questions to be answered, i.e. the quality of the course results and the means of effective measurement,
- assessment of the evaluation opportunities presented and the available methods in the specific situation,
- study of the findings in relation to the effect of the prevailing occasional factors,
- reflection on the evaluation process and on the findings of the study for future actions.

CAL is not solely a technological approach in learning, and it therefore should not be evaluated individually. CAL cost estimates include a fairly separate and complex set of issues, and no attempt is made to include them in the SECAL framework. The initial focus is on how CAL technology can improve the quality of learning outcomes in the short and long term to help make educational and social changes.

4.1.3.9 Hubbard Evaluation Framework

The Hubbard framework (Hubbard, 2011) includes four different purposes for evaluating CALL (Computer-Assisted Language Learning) applications: choice for use in a lesson, choice for use in self-access environments or for other instructors, and feedback during the development process. Hubbard presents these goals not as a complete list but as a specific subset in which its context can be applied.

Hubbard reduced the list of evaluation approaches or methodologies to three specific types: checklists, methodological frameworks, and SLA (second language acquisition) research. Checklists are essentially a combination of criteria reviewed by evaluators that define a type of score using either the Likert scale or other evaluation systems. While this is a common methodology used to evaluate CALL applications, in many cases it assumes that evaluation criteria are one-size-fits-all (size that fits everywhere). The evaluators can change or modify a checklist to match the criteria set by stakeholders, but the use of checklists as an approach or methodology for evaluating CALL applications may be confused with its overlap with the evaluation criteria. These checklists tend to be evaluation criteria lists and may not provide adequate methodological concerns for CALL evaluation, omitting key procedures in the evaluation process.

The other two approaches mentioned are not excluded from similar phenomena. The methodological frameworks, as described by Hubbard, allow evaluators to formulate their own questions. This may be a limitation for low-value appraisal evaluators based on CALL ratings like this, to guide their evaluation. Thus, it would be easier for evaluators to neglect potential stakeholders.

While the confusion between Hubbard's criteria and methodologies is not as strong as with checklists, evaluators can formulate their suggestions as defined criteria. Finally, SLA approaches seem to focus on methodologies and criteria on foreign language learning issues. Once again, it seems that the criteria and methodologies are being grouped. It is clear that there is a relationship between the evaluation criteria and the evaluation methodologies. However, a flexible evaluation framework for CALL applications should separate them to allow more options for evaluators when evaluating a CALL application.

Hubbard stated that the description of the frame reflected the purpose to choose a teacher to use in the classroom. Hubbard's processes include steps such as: delivering a technical preview, creating a functional description, assessing the adaptation of the instructor and trainee, forming appropriate views, and implementing plans.

In view of the above, the quality of the evaluation may be limited because the important steps in the evaluation process are not clearly stated, including examining the values of those concerned and describing the clear evaluation criteria. In addition, its context is often related to the evaluation of CALL courses and websites.

Hubbard did not specifically address the various stakeholders that may need to be considered when evaluating a CALL application. However, other stakeholders referred to Hubbard's CALL methodology, the evaluation of which is only one section. The three sections – development, implementation and evaluation – interact with each other, which can offer more interactions with those interested. However, in terms of the assessment unit, Hubbard initially focused on teachers and students. One reason given, the development of feedback during development, implies the assessments of CALL developers in an evaluation but does not include other potential stakeholders such as parents. In addition, School administration and staff are not mentioned as potential stakeholders, both of which are important because of their responsibility to fund and implement CALLs. In short, the Hubbard framework may be a good start to evaluating language learning programs or websites, but its uniqueness may limit its effectiveness for evaluators with different evaluation purposes, stakeholders, and criteria. A CALL evaluation framework should be broad enough to guide potential CALL evaluators in a variety of situations and purposes. Hubbard's framework may be a good start to evaluating language-learning educational programs or websites, but its specificity may limit its effectiveness for assessors with different assessment purposes, stakeholders, and criteria. A CALL evaluation framework should be broad enough to guide potential CALL evaluators in a variety of situations and purposes. Hubbard's framework may be a good start to evaluating language-learning educational programs, but its specificity may limit its effectiveness for the evaluators with different assessment purposes, stakeholders, and criteria. A CALL evaluation framework should be broad enough to guide potential CALL evaluators in a variety of situations and purposes.

4.1.3.10 Chappelle Evaluation Framework

Chappelle's (2001) evaluation framework is different from the Hubbard's model. From the beginning, it does not limit the types of evaluators as strictly as Hubbard. Its scope is broad enough to look at CALL software, CALL activities designed by teachers and student performance during CALL activities. It also records standards for the selection of evaluation criteria and even suggests some specific criteria. Chapelle (2001) examined the importance of criteria based on SLA research and stated that "language learning should be the main criterion in CALL evaluation". It also records the student's adjustment, i.e. concentration, authenticity, the positive impact and practice as criteria to be considered in CALL evaluations.

Chapelle suggested that CALL evaluations should be considered from two perspectives: (1) a critical analysis of CALL software and activities and (2) an empirical analysis of student performance. In many ways, this could be a recommendation for a variety of research methodologies. The evaluator orchestrates, at least to some extent, the type of analysis to be done in the evaluation.

Although some CALL evaluators seem to better evaluate, both qualitatively and quantitatively, this may be restrictive. Instead of relying on the type of approach of the evaluator, the framework should be based on a number of factors including the nature of the evaluator, the evaluation questions and the evaluation criteria.

The Hubbard and Chapelle frames differ in the focus point, with the Hubbard process emphasizing on the process, including its parts, details and specific suggestions for each step. For example, various purposes of a CALL evaluation are described. Chapelle, on the other hand, focused less on creating a process map for evaluations and more on purpose, criteria, and methodologies.

In summary, the Chapelle framework may be effective in some cases, especially those that assess CALL for language issues, but may not be useful when considering other non-SLA issues. Evaluators, examining non-SLA-related issues, such as finance, infrastructure or other administrative aspects, will benefit from a framework that includes other issues such as financial issues or hardware requirements. Following the Chapelle's framework, evaluations can also be created by not taking into account the values of those who are not adequately represented such as software developers and program managers.

4.1.3.11 M3: Three-Level Framework for Mobile Education Assessment

The M3 assessment framework was developed on the basis of Myartspace[8] (which combines classroom learning in combination with remote museums) and followed Lifecycle's approach to evaluating the educational technology (Vavoula and Sharples, 2009).The Lifecycle approach can be combined with a sequential system development process, with evaluations performed at the end of each stage, or with repetitive or socio-diagnostic methods (Vavoula and Sharples, 2009) where evaluation activities are carried out in key points that are very important to support the design process or to inform stakeholders. The evaluation with M3 is carried out at three levels:

1. *Micro Level,* which examines the individual activities of technology users and evaluates the usefulness and usefulness of the educational technology system. For Myartspace, the activities included collecting objects through code reports, recording notes, contacting students having collected a particular item, recording audio and taking photos.

2. *Learn Level,* which examines the learning experience as a whole in order to identify learning discoveries and analyzes. It also assesses how well the learning experience is integrated with other related activities and experiences. For Myartspace, the assessment at this level includes investigating the existence of a successful link between learning in the museum and that in the classroom,

---

[8] https://www.myartspace.com.sg/

as well as identifying critical incidents that reveal new standards and forms of learning or whether learning is hindered.

3. *Macro Level,* which examines the impact of new technology on established teaching and learning techniques and institutions. Assessment at this level examines the availability of new technology by teachers, the emergence of new practices, and how this can be related to the original vision of the project.

Myartspace's development included four broad phases: (1) analysis of requirements, definition of requirements for the socio-technical system (users and their interactions with technology) and determination of how it would work with the various stakeholders, (2) planning the user experience and the interface, (3) implementation of the service and (4) development of the service.

The emphasis on the level of requirements analysis changes during the process. At the beginning of a project, the requirements analysis must take into account all levels to set the initial requirements for an educational experience that incorporates technology, effective learning and institutional support. As the project progresses, the technology matures so that changes in requirements focus on learning. At the end of the project, the requirements have been finalized and evaluated at all levels. The emphasis on the evaluation level also changes during the development process. The first assessments at the micro level inform the user interface and the interactions between people and technology. Once the technology is strong enough to allow the evaluation of educational value, evaluation activities are introduced at the meso level during the implementation phase. Similarly, the macro level requires technology to be in place and used for a long time to demonstrate its impact on, for example, museum school practice practices, so that macro level assessment activities can be used. introduced during the development phase.

To determine the value of the service at each of the three levels, evaluation activities explore the gap between expectations and reality and reveal unpredictable processes and outcomes. This applies to both the data collection stage and the analysis stage.

1. *Stage 1:* data collection pertaining to what needs to happen at one level. User expectations at each level can be recorded through interviews with users (i.e. instructors, students, museum staff) and by analyzing the requirements of technical specifications, user documentation, training sessions and teaching materials.

2. *Stage 2:* data collection pertaining to what really happened on a level. The user experience is documented through observations and video and audio recordings to determine the actual use of the technology for different users.

3. *Stage 3:* examines the gap between expectations of use and reality through a combination of reflexive interviews with users and critical analysis of data collected in phases 1 and 2.

In summary, the M3 follows a Lifecycle continuous evaluation strategy approach to guide a flexible software development approach and inform stakeholders about the development process. It evaluates the evolving design and implementation at the three levels, utility, educational efficiency and institutional adoption. For each level, the assessment is related to what needs to happen (through interviews with stakeholders and examining records) to what is really going on (through user experience observation) and examines any gaps between expectation and reality as evidence of the need for modification. requirements, design, implementation or development.

The M3 provides a structured form for evaluating the usefulness, educational and organizational impact and relationships between them.

4.2 Evaluation Framework for Adaptive Systems

Adaptive systems become better known as software taking access to the information based on the user. This has led to offering a high degree of user satisfaction in different environments. For this reason, the effective and thorough evaluation of adaptive systems is particularly important. It is important not only to simply evaluate such systems but also to ensure that evaluation uses the right methods as a wrong method can lead to wrong conclusions.

The evaluation of interactive adaptive and personalized e-learning systems is very difficult, complicated and demanding due to the complex nature of these systems as adaptive interfaces dynamically change their content and layout according to each user's preferences and personal needs.

4.2.1 Evaluation Framework for End User Adaptation Systems (EFEx)

EFEx Goals and Functions
Evaluation Framework for End-user in Adaptive Systems (EFEx) has been designed as an online interface that allows users to collaborate and support the user in the following (Mulwa et al., 2011):

1. the search for relevant research material such as user-centered evaluation (UCE) studies and articles describing in detail the evaluation of similar adaptive systems,

2. take recommendations on how to best combine different evaluation methods, metrics and measurement criteria so that he can better evaluate his system,

3. identify a user-centered evaluation (UCE) methodology that describes how to apply existing UCE techniques,

4. translate the entire user interface into its language. EFEx supports 49 different languages.

When searching for relevant research material or evaluation recommendations, the user should be provided with the following features of a system: (system name, developer, the evaluation approach used, the purpose of the evaluation, the system description, the application area, the methods – evaluation – techniques used, evaluation metrics, evaluation criteria, the year the evaluation was conducted and what was improved with the adaptation).

Technical Application
EFEx is designed as a standard three-level architecture consisting of:

a. the level of presentation, which is the highest level of the application displaying information related to the services, such as browsing. It communicates with other levels by exporting results at the browser/client level and at all levels of the network,

b. the level of business logic extracted from the level of presentation and controls the functionality of an application by performing detailed processing, and

c. the level of data retention which keeps data independent of application servers or business logic. Giving data their own level improves scalability and performance. This architecture consists of:

- A pool with current evaluation techniques for user-centered adaptive systems. This interface allows users to search for:
  - ○ adaptive system evaluation studies focusing on the user,
  - ○ evaluation studies of models for adaptive systems (i.e. user, work, sector, strategy, content, device, system, navigation and strategy model).
- Provide recommendations to users to identify and apply the most appropriate methodologies and metrics:
  - ○ Recommendations for the evaluation of adaptive systems (i.e. system name, system purpose, system functions, application sector, evaluation methods, evaluation criteria, analysis and data type framework used) and
  - ○ Recommendations for evaluating model adaptive systems (i.e. model name, model purpose, model functions, application area, evaluation methods, criteria and evaluation metrics).
- A methodology that illustrates or explains how to apply user-centered evaluation techniques (UCE) (i.e. the results that have emerged after researching the properties and capabilities that UCE techniques can discover or evaluate).
- User modeling controller that handles the user registration process (i.e. username, password, email address and organizations) and (authentication). User registration is required before users can access the framework's recommendations.
- Translation section: the user interface translates into the language chosen by the user.
- The user interface controller which consists of the presentation of metrics and user interface controls.

The framework also provides features such as:

- A search point that will allow users to search and view the pool of all existing techniques and studies for user-centric evaluation for adaptive systems since 2000.
- An indirect recommendation algorithm that allows users to provide recommendations for identifying and applying the most appropriate methodologies and metrics.
- The specifications of the design and structure of adaptive systems.
- A set of elements (sections) that allow the execution of the evaluation methodology with a focus on the user.

The Target Audience

Final users of the EFEx framework can be categorized into two groups:

1. those who develop adaptive technologies/systems and want to control their results in end users,
2. those who develop adaptive experiences using adaptive technologies/systems.

Use Cases Scenario

Let's suppose that a developer has implemented an adaptive system. The user wants to use the EFEx framework to get recommendations on how to evaluate a custom system.

First, the users must register (i.e. user name, institution or organization, email address, password). They are provided with a form to complete (i.e. their system name, function, application area, evaluation method, evaluation criteria used, data types, system purpose and content used) and then they submit it. The EFEx framework examines the system and decides on the appropriate evaluation objectives. Based on the choice of the end users for the evaluation of the objectives, the framework proposes evaluation techniques for these users and provides explanations on how to apply these techniques. The users can also see evaluation research on user-centered adaptive systems and other existing studies on adaptive evaluation models.

Finally, let's assume that a user only speaks another language and not English. The EFEx framework provides personalized information according to the user's requirements based on his interests and preferences. This personalized e-learning experience uses an active learning strategy that allows the learner to have control over the overall context, pace, and extent of their learning experience.

Possible Educational and Industrial Benefits of the EFEx Framework
Evaluating adaptive systems is a demanding and complex task. For example, a major problem is understanding the system's customization mechanism. More specifically, it is difficult to show what was improved with the adjustment and what the situation might have been have a different adjustment. In addition, several researchers have emphasized the difficulties caused by the complexity of such systems and the issues of ease of use that arise (Chu et al., 1995).

This framework therefore provides users with: i) a central repository that stores current UCE studies of these systems, models and adaptive writing technologies. It is currently very difficult for evaluators and researchers to find this information in a central database and the report of these studies seems to be disordered. ii) personalized recommendations. These recommendations reduce the time wasted and the cost of evaluating these systems, models and technologies. Researchers can collaborate as they are distributed worldwide and learn faster.

4.2.2   Assessment Framework for Adaptive Supervisors

Although there are several frameworks for evaluating Adaptive Hypermedia Systems (AHS), recently proposed frameworks have been shown to be useful in determining the exact cause of failure or any other system failure. The framework proposed by (Gupta, 2004) treats evaluation as an integral part of an AHS development process and also evaluates the successful access of AHS to the Internet.

The proposed framework is an extension of evaluation frameworks using levels and these levels need to be evaluated in relation to other dimensions. The benefits of the framework are: a) it allows a structured, multi-level view to better understand the various aspects of AHS, b) it can be used as a conceptual framework for evaluating existing approaches to AHS, c) it can be used in development of the next generation AHS using software technology steps.

The framework consists of four dimensions – Environment, Adaptation, Development Process, and Evaluation Modules. All evaluation units must deal with all the components of the environment and the adaptation during each phase of the development process.

Environment

The first dimension, the environment, is the set of conditions to which AHS must adapt. They can be many different variables that affect the environment. They are grouped based on the following elements:

- **Device:** The advent of devices with limited web usage capabilities such as PDAs and mobile phones along with desktops – have made a paradigm of a size as well as the range of hardware and software is very wide. AHS should be evaluated for the proper acquisition of device features and smooth operation with hardware features such as screen sizes, local storage size, input methods, processing speed and software features such as browser versions, available add-ons, Java, Javascript, etc.

- **User:** Towards providing personalization, many AHS use the user's personal characteristics such as demographics, user knowledge, skills and abilities of the user, his/her interests and preferences, goals and plans. Along with these features, AHS should be evaluated for customization according to all users including people with disabilities and the elderly.

- **Application Sector:** AHS can be developed for a wide range of applications that differ in features. The specific features of the application are the critical parameters when evaluating AHS and should be evaluated together with the general characteristics of AHS as traditional concerns change depending on the field of application.

- **Position:** Information about the geographical location of the access device can be used to filter and customize or suggest the content of the AHS and must be evaluated for proper delivery.

Adjustment

The second dimension of the framework is the adaptation, which can be of two types: static adjustment and dynamic adjustment, depending on the time and the adjustment process. Static adjustments are determined by the author at the time of design or are specified only once at the start of the application. Dynamic adjustment is made during the interaction with the software depending on various factors such as user input, changes in user model, adjustment decisions taken by AHS, etc.

Evaluation Units

The third dimension of the evaluation framework consists of evaluation units which must be taken into account for the evaluation of AHS. These units have been proposed in frameworks using levels. A good perspective is to evaluate them in relation to the other dimensions of the framework.

- **Obtaining Entry:** Inputs from the environment as well as from the user are required. These can be obtained manually (i.e. the user can power them), automatically (i.e. the system can take the input itself, e.g. device type, screen size, location, etc.) or semi-automatically (i.e. some input through the user, some automatically).
  The inputs received by the system – either manually or automatically cannot hold any important information, but must be evaluated for reliability, accuracy, rate of sampling acquisition so that the conclusions drawn are useful.
  This must be done at all stages of the development phase – analysis, design,

implementation and maintenance, both for static and dynamic adaptations, for all devices, users, locations and application areas.

- **Drawing Conclusions:** The previous level included data collection, this level gives meaning to them, i.e. draws conclusions from them. The evaluators should check that these conclusions drawn by the system regarding user-computer interactions are correct, as it is not necessary that there be a direct mapping one by one between the first data and the corresponding important ones.

  In addition, entries given by different users from different devices or application areas may require different interpretations. The evaluators need to test whether all of these interpretations have been analyzed, designed, and applied in AHS for both static and dynamic adaptations.

- **Models:** To achieve the required adjustments, many models are created by the system. These models are based on the conclusions drawn at the previous stage and are supposed to mimic the real world. They must be evaluated for validity, i.e. the correct presentation of the entity being modeled, the completeness of the model, the content of the model, the accuracy of the model and the sensitivity of the modeling process.

- **Customization Decision:** Given a set of properties in the user model, sometimes there may be more adjustments. In this component, the evaluation of the most optimal adjustment is done with criteria such as the necessity of the adjustment, the suitability of the adjustment and its acceptance. Careful evaluation is required to check if the increase in adjustment does not result in a reduction in usability.

- **Presentation:** This unit includes human-computer interaction and should be evaluated for criteria such as presentation consistency, presentation completeness, timely customization, and user control for customization.

Development Process

The fourth dimension of the framework is the development process that includes the phases of the software life cycle, i.e. analysis, design, implementation and maintenance.

During each phase of this dimension, the evaluation of the individual elements of the environment, the evaluation and adaptation units is carried out in relation to the others.

- **Analysis**

  This phase involves gathering information about the problems of the current system and/or identifying the requirements and limitations of the system to be developed. Key elements of this phase are:

  ○ *Function analysis:* determines the basic functions that are expected to be performed and how they are performed.

  ○ *Environmental analysis:* analyzes the environment that is expected to be accessed by the system, including physical parameters such as location, device and other aspects such as application area and user type.

  ○ *User and job analysis:* determines the scope of cognitive characteristics such as user preferences, goals, knowledge and other characteristics required in the user model e.g. search strategy etc. required.

  ○ *Interface analysis:* identifies features such as efficiency, learning ability, flexibility and behavior required by the system.

  ○ *Data analysis:* includes the input acquisition analysis to locate data to be stored and managed by the system, and the understanding and representation of the importance and structure of data in AHS.

◦ *Model Analysis:* includes the analysis of various models kept in the system such as the user model, the sector model, the navigation model, the customization model.

In order to evaluate this phase, checklists can be prepared for the different types of analysis mentioned earlier, which correspond to a variety of elements of different dimensions of the evaluation framework. For example, a checklist is prepared for the functional requirements of static customization for computer input, another checklist for PDAs for the same specifications.

- **Design**
  The design phase defines the overall organization of the system by transforming the functions and tasks defined during the analysis phase into software elements and the externally visible properties of these elements as well as their relationship. It is recommended to design the adaptive parts of the system in parallel with the whole system so that a successful adaptation is achieved. Some elements of this phase are:

  ◦ *Architectural design:* Many architectural designs for adaptive systems have been proposed.
    In this model, the unit of acquisition of users' input take the data entry by the user through the keyboard or mouse or from other external factors such as the device and the access location of the AHS. This input is verified and then transferred to the next unit "Drawing conclusions" to infer logical conclusions which are stored in some dynamic models created by the system, such as the user model. The "modeling" unit consists of several models – both static and dynamic, such as the user model, the sector model, the navigation model, the presentation model and the custom model. Different AHS may have one or more such models used at different levels of adaptation. Depending on some models, the "adaptation decision" unit makes the decision to select the best customization techniques available to the system. Then, the "presentation" unit presents the final content and links to the user.
    The evaluation of architectural design is important because it determines the limitations in implementation and maintenance, making it easier to justify and manage changes and determines the quality characteristics of the system.

  ◦ *Content design:* Content is one of the most important aspects of AHS, as AHS exists because of its content. Therefore, its accuracy must be verified. In addition, the content that will be visible to different users (depending on their individual user model), on different devices and location needs to be identified and evaluated.

  ◦ *Navigation design:* Since there are many navigation techniques (such as direct navigation, hiding links, etc.) that can be used with a variety of navigation aids such as icons, graphics, we need to make sure that the selected technique is appropriate for the content and accordingly with heuristics leading to high quality interface designs and also ensuring that aids (such as location maps and table of contents) are designed within the system.

Evaluating the navigation design is necessary to ensure that the integrity of the entire system is maintained as the user moves into the application as long as it is related to the communication performance of the AHS.

○ *Interface design:* As the user interface is the "first impression" of the system, a poorly designed interface can disappoint the user regardless of the value of the content, the complexity of the architectural design and the navigation techniques used. Therefore, careful evaluation is required for well-structured and ergonomic interface designs.

The design phase can be evaluated using metrics such as structural complexity measurement, navigation metrics, utility, etc.

- **Implementation**
  During the actual implementation of the system, the evaluation of each AHS unit must be done individually and then integrated with the other units for successful adjustment at different levels – both statically and dynamically, for different users, on different devices. Some metrics, such as behavioral complexity, reliability metrics, accuracy, software size, and length measurements, help evaluate the system as a whole. In addition, the evaluation of the tools can be done in relation to the activities in which they are used to indicate their availability for each type of activity and the way in which the tool supports it.
- **Maintenance**
  AHS may require updating at any time. Therefore, during the design phase, care must be taken to design the spaceframe (hyperspace) in a modular way so that the change of structure can be done by changing the relationships between these units. Automatic link creation should be preferred over static links to maintain link coherence. Maintaining static links is complicated as any change to a node location in the hyperlink makes it necessary to review all documents that include links to this node in order to update them.

  Content maintenance can be made easily by storing content separately from the structure of the main idea or navigation options, as the content is external and can be easily updated. Finally, the database should be used to store information about different parts of the system, in order to facilitate the management and maintenance of this data and to ensure the coherence of the data. The checklists can be prepared for them and the measurements can be used to measure the ease of maintenance, such as metric complexity, reuse metrics or extensibility metrics.

  During the development of an adaptive teaching system for the internet, during the implementation phase, the accuracy of the content is measured for the presentation unit. The values are supplemented using different metrics that are suitable for the different stages and can be in any unit of measurement. For a complete evaluation, many such tables will be required for the different phases.

The proposed evaluation framework incorporates the AHS development process, the access environment, the different types and levels of adaptation involved in AHS and the framework evaluation units. Several factors that affect the evaluation of AHS can be organized around these contextual perspectives. The framework is a mechanism for acquiring knowledge and understanding of AHS for the internet. It can be used for summary evaluations after the completion of AHS by replacing the "growth process" with the "initial goals and objectives achieved" and controlling them with the other dimensions. It can also be used for configuration evaluations during system development, setting goals for each phase and then comparing the actual results.

4.3   Assessment Framework for Educational Games

Games are the most popular digital activity for children, especially as applications in mobile devices. One of the most special advantages of educational digital games for children is their ability to positively influence their attitude towards learning (Troussas et al., 2020 (d)). This can happen due to several factors:

- Graphics, sound and movement can attract children's interest more than text and photos in books.
- The challenge and competition experienced by the games can further promote the educational content offering enthusiasm to users in comparison to the static nature of the non-interactive media.
- Random access and parallel processing are an innate characteristic of young children, who inherently have a short attention span.
- Immediate reward is an incentive to persevere, which is more important for young children than long-term rewards.
- The low level of threat associated with game failure creates self-confidence and positively affects the child to a better learning experience.
- Imagination and storytelling characters attract young children to indulge in an emotional experience.

All of the above factors contribute to the fact that children prefer to spend more time playing games than studying using traditional means. The long period of time that children can spend playing games renders them an incredible learning opportunity. Touch screen devices allow children to interact with technology at a younger age. Very young children who have had problems using a mouse as an indirect indicator to hit a target or play with controls can now navigate with a touch screen intuitively and easily.

One of the main concerns associated with the GBL (Games-Based Learning) literature is the lack of empirical evidence to support the validity of the approach (De Freitas et al., 2010) stated that a key element that is missing is the ability to properly evaluate games for educational and training purposes. If games are not properly evaluated and there is no specific empirical evidence in individual learning scenarios that can produce generalized results, then the perspective of games on learning can always be dismissed as unfounded optimism. In the aforementioned study, much of the literature was collected and analyzed by information systems. The majority of studies have examined the performance analysis of game measurements.

While the lack of empirical evidence to support GBL is not a new issue, the growing popularity of gaming combined with recent developments in gaming and hardware technology, the advent of virtual worlds, and massively multiplayer online gaming (MMOG), reinforces the need for a flexible assessment. Following, evaluation frameworks for educational games are presented.

4.3.1 Pre-MEGa Evaluation Framework

With the proliferation of mobile gaming devices for preschoolers, there is a growing need for high-quality gaming for this age group. But how can quality be defined? The goal is to find an entertaining, useful, educational and above all successful game. The framework presented (Shoukry et al., 2015) aims to facilitate the process of translating research into specific, measurable features for the design and evaluation of this type of software.

The evaluation framework proposed aims to facilitate the process of designing and evaluating educational games for mobile devices for preschool children, providing an easy-to-use list that combines the parts that fit the category from different systems. The framework was divided into the following 15 categories: (1) screen design, (2) navigation and control, (3) ease of use, (4) responsiveness, (5) game design, (6) learning ability, (7) instructions, (8) feedback, (9) difficulty level, (10) content presentation, (11) pedagogical factor, (12) adaptation, (13) security, (14) accessibility and (15) value.

The Pre-MEGa framework consists of the aforementioned categories of guidelines for designing a successful mobile educational game for preschoolers. It can be used for both designing and evaluating this category of software and covers areas of learning, usability and play, taking into account the specific age group and aspects of the touch screen of mobile devices.

Using the Pre-MEGa Framework
First, it can be used to determine specific design requirements. As most of the time it is not possible to meet all the requirements of the framework, this step follows a set of design objectives. A useful model, in this respect, is the PLU-E framework which is based on the PLU model. Using this framework, the designer or evaluator determines the percentage for each of the three variables, P (Playing), L (Learning) and U (Using) to map the product to the model. PLU and determine accordingly the appropriate evaluation method.

In summary, the Pre-MEGa framework is intended to be used as a theoretical basis that summarizes previous research and is updated with new trends that can be further evaluated, improved and adapted to different specifications and target users.

4.3.2 PLU-E Evaluation Framework

As there are many models that support the design process of a software development project, the evaluation process is not very well-defined and this lack of definition often leads to poorly designed evaluations or the use of incorrect evaluation method. Children's product reviews can be very complex, as they have to look at different requirements and goals that such a product may have and often use new or evolving evaluation methods. Evaluations should be planned from the beginning of a project in order to achieve the best results and suggest a framework to facilitate this.

The PLU model is a pre-existing model designed to help understand and determine how children interact with technology. This model defines three different relationships that children have with interactive products, which roughly record the three types of interactive technology. In this model, children are described as Players, Students or Users and technologies are described as Entertainment, Education and Activation. In the PLU (Playing, Learning, Using) model, a product and the child's purpose can be mapped to a three-dimensional space and the distance between these mappings can to some extent predict a mismatch between the designers' perceptions of technology and experience.

The proposed PLU-E framework is described below:

1. *Decide on the purpose and focus of the product*, both in terms of project objectives and PLU. It concerns how entertaining is a tutoring system and how educationally beneficial is a game. This may have already been addressed to some extent with some specification requirements or a project proposal.
   - Are there parts of it (e.g. specific interaction techniques/interface parts, etc.) that are particularly challenging and therefore need to be addressed as a matter of priority?

2. *Identify key users and special users.*
   - Are these distinct user groups to be treated separately, or are all users part of the same group?

3. *Based on steps 1 and 2, the project team agrees with the weighing of the PLU they consider to represent the product.* The team must agree to what extent the proposed product aims to support the game, learning or use (Playing, Learning or Using correspondingly). For example, an educational game for a typical group of children can be [P: 35%, L: 50%, U: 15%] – product goals are weighed higher for learning but still require fun.

4. *Decide at what points tests (evaluations) should be performed.*
   a. It is expected that the evaluations will be "guided by the characteristics", using original or existing products. The focus and key features identified in stage 1 will be examined individually (e.g. if the product is a tangible game, an evaluator can examine the usefulness of the tangible interaction, while another evaluator can assess the entertainment degree of the game, etc.), to lead to the final design of the product. It can also be clarified that the data from these tests will be used for the project flow.
   b. After checking the components of the product, the project will enter an original phase, the extent of which may vary depending on the limitations of the project (e.g. this may include a flash version of the software, after a full application of basic screens and so on, alternatively it can be a complete application from scratch with some incomplete features that will be added in later stage).
   c. A "final check" of the final product should be scheduled at some point before the end of the project, giving time to solve the problems (if the purpose of the project is its development), or to analyze the problems (if the purpose of the project is to investigate the process).

5. *Based on stages 3 and 4 and project constraints (e.g. user time and availability), evaluations can be scheduled.*
   a. For example, focus on usefulness may mean using the evaluation methods that control it, such as expert inspection methods (utility specialists, developmental psychologists, etc.) and user testing. Entertainment is likely to be evaluated through user testing, self-assessment and observations. The evaluation of learning can be done better through evaluation by learning experts (e.g. teachers, educational psychologists, etc.).

b. Each test in the process (as defined in step 4) will need to reconsider steps 1, 2 and 3, leading to different ratings selected at this stage. Each test should determine the most appropriate form of evaluation for the particular piece (e.g. the usefulness of a tangible game could be addressed through a heuristic evaluation or ergonomic testing of tangible components, while entertainment could be examined through observations). An important question to be asked is whether it would be annoying for users to check the product (or part of it) at each stage.

c. The final test should reflect the level of PLU produced at stage 3: e.g. a product that is primarily intended to be entertaining should be evaluated mostly for how much fun it is.

Finally, the overall goal of this framework is to always design evaluations based on product goals, so that evaluators can obtain the best possible data for their time, hoping that this can then lead to a smoother design process for developers, and ultimately a better designed product for all users.

4.3.2.1 *Methodological Framework for the Evaluation of Educational Games*

The proposed methodological framework by Antoniou et al. (2011) examines and uses knowledge from the field of cognitive psychology to evaluate aspects of educational games. Specifically, they focused on two components of human knowledge that play a central role in learning, namely memory and motivation. After reviewing the theories in this area, the authors created a questionnaire to evaluate educational games. The questionnaire includes different experimental findings of cognitive psychology. In particular, they applied Maslow's theory of motivation, behavioral outcomes, and experimental findings on attention and memory.

A methodology for evaluating such applications should be able to allow for easy evaluation of the product's range of functionality ("Can the user effectively do what s/he intends to do?"), the impact of the interface ("Is the product easy to use?"), and identifying problems (Dix and Talis, 2016). For this reason, they have developed a methodology that combines different evaluation methods in a novel way. Specifically, the proposed methodology is the combination and extension of inspection methods and analysis models. According to the classification proposed by Ivory and Hearst (2001), there are different methods that can be used to evaluate different applications.

In the past, there have been research efforts in the direction of cognitive assessment of video games. Specifically, Gackenbach and Rosie (2009) asked game players to reliably evaluate different games, based on the PASS model, which examines different aspects of human knowledge (Planning, Attention, Simultaneous and Successive cognitive processing). The results revealed the importance of cognitive assessment of games. However, the methodology used was time-consuming, both in terms of data collection and statistical analysis. Undoubtedly, such an approach will produce significant results based on user perceptions. However, there are some cases where time and resource constraints require methodologies that can produce useful results in a less time-consuming way. For this purpose, the proposed methodology only concerns the evaluation of games based on cognitive principles by experts.

Cognitive Discoveries (Inspection Method) and Cognitive Work Analysis (Analysis Model) were combined to create a methodology in which experts use and evaluate educational games. Based on theories of cognitive psychology, a questionnaire was developed to summarize the key findings and give an easy picture of the results. The questionnaire is easy to use and can produce fast and quality results. A quick look at the results may reveal potential areas for improvement.

The Questionnaires
A first limited form of questionnaire will be presented as an example of the proposed method. All questions come from cognitive and behavioral theories about human motivation and memory. From the findings on human memory, the questionnaire includes the following questions:
- Do the features of the game attract the player's attention to the desired points?
- Is there audio encoding?
- Is there semantic coding? (for example, a small sword on a button could symbolize the player's available weapons in the game).
- Is there visual coding? (Is the environment organized in a way that is essential for the players?).
- Are there up to 7 ± 2 units of information or groups of objects available to the user? (more units can lead to a cognitive overload).
- Can information be retrieved through recognition or recollection? (recognition of information is less demanding than memory).
- What is the volume of data or information that the user handles?
- Is there any interference? (optical or audio).
- Can the player practice or repeat the required information or skill?
- Are there help options and non-player characters? To what extent?

From the findings on human motivation, the questionnaire includes the following questions:
- Are there clear rules?
- It is safe; Or does the player perceive it as safe?
- Does it make the player feel like he's going somewhere?
- Is there a sense of appreciation?
- Is it easy to understand and impart knowledge to players?
- What is the aesthetics of the game?
- Does it cover the player's needs for self-esteem?
- Does it have positive incentives? What kind of;
- Are there penalties? What kind of?
- Are there balanced incentive ratios? (encouragement schedule).
- Are there balanced breaks between incentives?

Finally, the proposed methodological framework is by no means complete, as only two areas of human knowledge are used. In the future, we plan to add findings from other areas of cognition, such as language, vision, etc.

In summary, although questionnaires are used in this model, the technique remains high qualitative, providing indications of positive, negative or even neutral characteristics of the games, instead of giving a final degree to the games.

In view of the above, questionnaires summarize the key features of games and help the evaluation process. The tables provide a structured environment for visualizing the results, thus helping the evaluator and aiming at key points that should not be overlooked.

In addition, the tables are easy to use and self-explanatory to be understood. Their use is flexible and can cover a wide range of different games, such as educational games, simple or more complex games, etc. The questions used are based on well-known theories of human knowledge. The proposed methodology is also easy to use and can help game evaluators aim at different elements of the game. Finally, according to Dix and Talis (2016), the evaluation process should be part of a comprehensive product development cycle, and not just something that is done in the end. In this light, the proposed methodology can serve as a development tool (i.e. to provide guidelines to developers) as well as a tool for final evaluation, allowing to conclude that there seem to be cognitive and behavioral reasons for the success or failure of different games.

4.3.3   Game Object Model Version II (GOM II)

Complex computer games can be a means, based on appropriate theoretical concepts, to transform the educational environment. Based on the original game object model (GOM) (Amory, 2007), a more detailed model is developed that supports concepts that educational games, on a computer, must include:

- be relevant, exploratory, emotional, riveting and include complex challenges, to support authentic learning activities, designed as narrative social spaces where learners are transformed through exploration of multiple representations and thinking,
- include the gender dimension, to provide appropriate standards,
- develop democracy, and social capital through dialogue supported by computer communication tools, and include challenges, puzzles or questions, which form the core of the learning process, where access to clear knowledge, discussions and reflection results in the acquisition of tacit knowledge.

It is argued that version II of the GOM can be used not only to support the development of educational games but also to provide a mechanism for evaluating the use of computer games in the classroom.

The GOM Model

It was originally presented by Amory (2007), and describes the relationship between pedagogical dimensions of learning and game elements and relies on the example of Object-Oriented Programming which includes concepts such as encapsulation, heredity and polymorphism. The transfer of object-oriented planning was chosen to support the development and analysis of complex plans and to facilitate the understanding of complex situations. While the design components of an educational game must be interconnected (interact with each other), and not be considered as a linear collection of functions, such objects should be considered as independent in the phase of design and development.

In GOM, Amory (2007) consider that an educational game consists of a number of objects, each of which is described by abstract and specific interfaces. Abstract interfaces refer to all pedagogical and theoretical constructions and the specific interfaces refer to the design of elements. Therefore, educational game designers use abstract interfaces in the game design phase while game developers realize these pedagogical aspects of an educational game by incorporating specific interfaces into game software and the game.

Items can be free or part of other items, so they inherit all parental interfaces. The internal objects (which inherit all parental interfaces) contain mainly specific interfaces (represented by open circles) while the external ones are more abstract (represented by closed circles). In GOM, the object Game Space includes the object Visualization Space which consists of the objects Elements Space and Problem Space. The Item Space item includes the Actor Space object.

The Game Space object includes four motivational abstract interfaces: play, exploration, challenge, and devotion (Rieber, 1996).

The Illustration Space object includes these interfaces related to cognitive activities such as critical thinking, discovery, goal creation, goal accomplishment, competition, practice (Amory, 2007) and includes this particular Story Line Interface.

The Item Data Space includes abstract entertainment (Malone, 1980) and specific interfaces of graphics, sound and technology and the interaction of carriers and movement (Amory, 2007).

The object Space of Problem includes the specific interfaces of handling, memory, mathematics, logic and reflexes (Amory, 2007) that perform the critical thinking, discovery, goal formation, goal completion and practice interface (Leutner, 2000).

Objectives

GOM II (theoretical concepts) includes a number of sub-domains: definition of computer games, authentic learning, storytelling, gender, social collaboration, and puzzle-goal challenges. Each of these subtopics includes theoretical structures and arguments, and key concepts derived from the theoretical discussions used to develop GOM II. Each section concludes with abstract and specific interfaces that emerge from the theoretical discussion.

The basic concepts mentioned above identify the new interfaces related to the GOM II framework. The new version maintains the Gaming Space, Image Space, Data Space, Body Space, and Problem Space of the original GOM model, but introduces a new Social Space object. In addition, the subject Problem Space now inherits from both the Image Space object and the Social Space (multiple heredity). Each object is examined separately.

The Game Space object includes only abstract game-related interfaces (play, exploration, challenges and dedication) and game design (narrative spaces, authenticity, multiple ideological views and gender integration) that result in Social Transformation) and development of silent knowledge (Tacit knowledge) (results of the game).

The specific interfaces of graphics, sound, technology, history and cut scenes contribute to the fun and emotionally abstract interfaces of the item Space Elements. The carrier object includes the abstract drama interface and the specific interaction, motion, and template interfaces. The Items Data Space and Body Space objects are closely related to the Story Space interface.

The Social Space object is introduced to support the development of online communities and to leverage technology-based social interaction the interfaces of democracy, social capital and dialogue. Computer Space includes Computer Mediated Communication (CMC) and Social Network Analysis (SNA). The CMC object supports discussions (dialogues) through the Network, and specific communication tool interfaces. Social capital includes Relationships, which can be Decentralized using SNA techniques and are therefore the specific interfaces of the SNA object.

The Object Space object is the most complex element of the model and includes all the interfaces of the Image Space and CMC objects. In addition, the Problem Space object (which includes mini-games, challenges, searches, and other "problems") includes abstract interfaces of embarrassment (questioning), adaptation, assimilation (related to puzzle design), and complexity, flow. and activity-related ones (puzzle interactions). Puzzles should include both win/lose solutions and indirect conflicts, explicit knowledge, discussions and rather the construction of models from the use of models (specific interfaces).

Therefore, GOM II consists of a number of complex interrelated objects (updated by modern educational theories and practices) used to describe educational games that could be simplified over three long periods (challenges, narration, and discussion). Educational games are therefore transformed devices in which the real challenges of problem solving, puzzles or questions are driven and supported by narrative devices and conversations. The model should be seen as a means of structuring discussions and could easily be reconsidered to suit different or alternative views.

Uses of GOM II
A simple way to use GOM II would be to create a checklist of all the necessary criteria (specific interfaces) and evaluate the game's design specifications in relation to that list. However, the viability and validity of the model when creating complex learning environments must be evaluated in practice.

McAllister (2004) suggests that game evaluators need to understand the relationship between mass culture, the media, psychosomatic, economic, and educational forces in industrial contradictions in order to "encourage transformational work in both the computer game complex and in races involved".

GOM II provides a mechanism for reviewing computer games from a learning perspective (learning versus teaching). Evaluating all the abstract interfaces would show the pedagogical adaptation of a particular game, while evaluating the specific interfaces would show how well a game achieves the educational goals. For example, The Sims[9], a popular game in recent years, would be rated very low on abstract conversion and multi-point interfaces as the game replicates consumer culture while most of Myst's[10] titles would be rated higher for these interfaces as games develop an understanding (knowledge) of other cultures. Although not all games include CMC, they could even be used in collaborative environments where more than one player could play a game on a computer. Nevertheless, developing a GOM II-based evaluation will require the development of self-assessment criteria.

4.3.4   Game-Based Learning Assessment

The research area Game-Based Learning (GBL) has attracted the interest of the scientific community; however, there is scope for a lot of improvements. The lack of frameworks for evaluating GBL is a key reason for limited empirical evidence to support the validity of this approach. The literature has a number of articles that suggest ways in which GBL can be evaluated with specific criteria with various experimental designs and analytical techniques (Troussas et al., 2020 (d)). Following, general guidelines related to researchers evaluating GBL environments with particular emphasis on student performance will be presented. The main idea for this kind of evaluation is to determine what can possibly

---

[9]   https://www.ea.com/games/the-sims
[10]   https://store.steampowered.com/app/63660/Myst_Masterpiece_Edition/

be evaluated in a GBL application. Like the four-dimensional framework (De Freitas et al., 2010) presented earlier, the categories should not necessarily be treated individually but as a collective set depending on what is to be evaluated. Such guidelines can be used in the development of GBL to update the design of an application and to show broad paradigms of individual analytical measurements of the stakeholders.

Progress and Performance of Learners

This category involves the pedagogical affordance from the learner's perspective and evaluates aspects of his/her progress and performance. The category deals primarily with whether there is an improvement in the student's performance as a result of the learning intervention. Improvements are especially linked to the learning outcomes of GBL intervention and can include: improving knowledge acquisition (procedural, declarative, general), formulating metacognitive strategies and improving skills formation, etc.

Motivation for Tutors and Students

This category deals primarily with the specific motivations of the learner to use the system as well as the level of his/her interest to participate in the learning process, the participation for an extended period of time and the determination of the specific motivations that are most important (Connolly et al., 2012). Do students participate directly and indirectly? Which specific features of the GBL environment or simulation are the most important? Is the learners' attention distracted in any way? Are they willing to include the GBL environment in the tutoring of other courses? Also looking at Kirkpatrick's four-level model for evaluating the effectiveness of the software, it is important to identify the motivations that apply not only to the student but also to the tutor. Therefore, it may be important to determine what motivates tutors to try to incorporate a GBL approach into their curricula.

Perceptions of Tutors and Students

This category mainly includes perceptions related to learners, such as their perception of time in a game, how real the game seems to be, and how it is related to plausible assumptions. The category also includes students' perceptions of how GBL intervention can help them and if they are confused between education and entertainment. The instructor will have similar perceptions depending on his/her particular involvement. If the instructor simply incorporates the content after the intervention or the GBL simulation then his/her perceptions may be more important than whether the intervention fits well in a particular context.

Attitudes of Tutors and Students (Behavior)

This category is mainly about the attitude of the tutors and students towards different elements that can change the effectiveness of the GBL intervention. These elements include: learners' attitudes towards the domain to be taught, learners' behavior towards gaming (Connolly et al., 2012), instructors' behavior towards integrating games into the educational process, and learners' behavior about several game elements, such as multimedia, sounds, colors, interface, consistency, feedback utility for learning a topic and achieving learning outcomes.

Preferences of Tutors and Students

This category refers to the preferences of the learner and the instructor during a GBL intervention. Learners prefer to learn in different ways of learning and therefore different learners will have different preferences. This category may include: preference of students about multimedia when receiving the tutoring by instructors, preference for conventional or GBL training, preference and use of specific game features, and preference for different competitive modes (Yu et al., 2001). For an instructor, this category could include the possibility to incorporate GBL intervention in their specific course or if they prefer to teach using GBL approaches.

Collaborative Support
This category is active only if the GBL application includes collaborative activities. However, it needs to be noted that collaboration offers pedagogical potential in educational systems. As mentioned, collaboration depends on whether the game is played on an individual level, on a collaborative team level, on a competitive team level or on multiple collaborative teams competing with each other. Collaboration can be assessed by exploring the ways to achieve learning outcomes, or specific goals.

GBL Environment and User Interface
This category includes all aspects that could be assessed regarding the GBL environment. It is a quite complex category since it can be divided into the following five subcategories: virtual environment, program frame creation, usability, level of social presence and development. Regarding the virtual environment itself, the evaluation criteria can be the following: confirmation of the background environment and characters including the expression of a virtual factor (Dugdale et al., 2006), evaluation of the factors in relation to the change of the environment, the importance of environmental advice, the context of the environment in terms of real-world decision making and the overall difficulty of the game.

Feedback, advice and resources in the environment are valuable to support the learner in achieving his/her learning outcomes. The framework of the program can be evaluated by monitoring the appropriate realism, feedback, the learner's perception of the quality of the advice, the expertise on the quality of the advice and monitoring the use of resources and advice. Utility can be analyzed by looking at specific work completion times, the average completion time (of an activity), the ease of work, the number of errors made during the execution of a task, and the classification of tasks by students.

Utility can also be assessed through conversation analysis, correlation of the learner's personal characteristics and cognitive capacity. It is also possible to monitor the gradual reactions of players in a repetitive way to assess aspects of usability. The level of social presence has to do with the interaction and immersion in the game world. It can be monitored by examining relationship frequencies, evaluating players' game personality traits, behavior and mood statements, and events in the game that indicate social presence.

Development aims to include the most effective method of integrating the GBL application into the educational context and may also involve the preference of different game conditions, i.e. a specific form of technical delivery and also about integrating the GBL environment into the curriculum.

4.3.5   RETAIN Evaluation Framework

The Relevance Embedding Transfer Adaptation Immersion and Naturalization (RETAIN) model developed by Gunter et al. (2008) is based on methods of interconnected teaching and learning theories. game design. The RETAIN model is based on six key aspects: relativity, integration, metaphor, adaptation, concentration, and acclimatization.

Relativity concerns three different aspects: (1) the learning materials that should be relevant to the students, their needs and the way of learning, (2) the teaching units that should be related to each other, i.e. the teaching modules should be introduced and regulated in relation to previous materials taught, and (3) the game should be relevant to reality, which includes information on how to use imagination, i.e. the fiction that is supported (with narration as commonly is in the games). A related aspect refers to the appropriately embedded content in the game's rationale. The intention is to integrate the educational content in such a way that it is inherent in the imaginary context of the game.

Knowledge transfer and adaptation are closely related. The first aspect refers to the ability to teach students (players) on how to transfer knowledge from one situation to another and can be achieved by stimulating memory. The second concerns the acquisition of knowledge and can be achieved through assimilation – interpretation of facts in relation to previously known facts – and modification – change or creation of new knowledge, expanding the understanding of players.

Concentration is the creation of a belief in the imaginary environment of the digital environment. It can be measured hierarchically by a simple interaction/reaction to complete commitment to the game. Adequate interaction and a high level of commitment (provided by well-designed games) favor concentration.

Escalation refers to automatic or spontaneous use of knowledge, in which the user uses the information he has learned regularly and permanently, monitors it, but does not need to devote time and gray matter to think about it. Games that can be played again, i.e. that the player enjoys playing many times, push into acclimatization.

To simplify the use of the framework, the creators defined a table that classifies each of the five aspects presented at four levels (from 0 to 3). Each level has its own requirements so that the game is considered at this level in a specific aspect. In a typical example, a game would be: level 1 in relativity, level 2 in integration, level 2 in metaphor, level 0 in adaptation, level 3 in concentration, and level 2 in acclimatization. In addition, the authors classified the importance of each aspect by defining the scale of the weighting. The table in combination with the scale can be used to guide the development of DLG (Digital Learning Games, Digital Learning Games) and to evaluate the effectiveness of an existing game.

Each of these aspects can be divided into four levels: 0, 1, 2, 3. Level 0 means that the design of the game does not correspond to this aspect, while level 3 shows that there is a strong correlation between the game and that of necessary aspect.

Intermediate lines show the gravity of each aspect. Gunter and his colleagues classified the aspects based on their importance. From the least important to the most important, they are: Relativity, Concentration, Integration, Adaptation, Transfer and Eligibility.

Analyzing this table, it is concluded that although the above games have a low score on the RETAIN model, they have an important place in learning environments. Their contribution to the introduction and practice of vocabulary and grammar contribute to language learning.

4.3.6   TEEM Evaluation Framework

The games selected for testing in the classroom were mainly those of simulation or search games. Some of them contained some arcade elements that often appeared randomly or as a reward for the successful completion of a task. Other types of games have not been identified as suitable for classroom use, although they may have some broader educational benefits in an informal learning environment

TEEM evaluation framework includes a series of questions and issues under the headings that are known to be important when evaluating software. Some questions may be unnecessary when writing about specific games. Nevertheless, regardless of the software, the purpose of the framework is the same. It is a document that presents a series of titles that teachers report on their scope and experience of a program and offer questions that need to be considered when writing about each of the specific topics – content, curriculum relevance, design and navigation, etc. When writing Teachers will have developed a sensitivity to the issues related to each section as they watch each game and then write about the title keeping these issues in mind. This ensures that there is a resemblance of information about the games being evaluated, allowing the evaluators to be properly compared.

1. **General picture of the use of this game in the classroom**
   We give a short summary of the game and how it can be used in the classroom.
   ○   What topics and goals of teaching and learning does the game support?
   ○   What are the possible features of this product for classroom use?
   ○   Where is this product better suited to the school context?
   ○   What do teachers need to know in order to use this product effectively?
   ○   What are the weaknesses of the product for classroom use?
   ○   What kind of computer use does this product support, i.e. the whole class in a computer room, a small group in a computer in the classroom, individual use, groups etc.?

2. **About the curriculum**
   Game software can be an indispensable tool for a classroom because it helps children develop skills about education, and/or engage with relevant curriculum content.

   a. Content
       – Is the relevant content sufficiently defined for classroom use? For example, is the relevant content easy to distinguish from the content of another game from which children are not required to learn?
       – Is there enough relevant content to justify the use of the game?
       – Is the layout of the content sufficiently accessible to justify its use?
       – Is the quality of the text acceptable? Examine the accuracy, relevance, and quality of images, video, and audio.
       – When the game simulates a real environment, do the laws governing the actions and the consequences, the behavior of the individual elements, follow the accepted models or the rules related to the same real state of the world?
       – Do the skills practiced in the virtual environment match those required in the natural environment?

b.   Skills

In addition to related skills, many games require the user to use strategic or sequential thinking, problem solving, and complex thinking skills to solve the puzzle or play the game. These may include making assumptions and testing them. Comment on the type of thinking strategy and skills you see that children need to follow to use the game. Some of these terms from the basic skills curriculum can be useful.

Contact – participating in group discussions, understanding and responding to others.

Application of numbers – computational skills, applying computational skills and understanding numbers in real-life situations.

Collaborate with others – to meet a challenge, to develop social skills and decision-making and decision-making skills.

Improving their own learning and performance – identifying ways to improve their learning and performance, identifying barriers and problems, discussing ways to improve learning.

Problem solving – identifying and understanding a problem, designing solutions, monitoring progress, reviewing problem solutions.

Financial ability – budget, expenses, savings, sharing, borrowing and efficiency.

Business education – risk management, learning from mistakes, innovation.

3. **Design and navigation**

Do program design and navigation support classroom use? The following are involved in the above question:
- Are the icons important and can be easily selected by clicking the mouse?
- Can you easily get in and out of the section you want? Can you put a bookmark on where you are, or record an individual user position so that they start again from where they left off?
- Is it clear how you move around the product?
- Is there a way to navigate back to the program?
- Where there are tasks for the player, is the score recorded somewhere?

4. **Ease of use**
- Can a child use the software with minimal help, either alone or with a peer?
- Is there a significant amount of time that needs to be spent to start the game – creating an environment, infrastructure before the game can be played? Are there any examples for the user to start?

5. **Edutainment (Education and Entertainment)**
- Are these exercises easily accessible?
- Do the exercises gradually become more difficult?
- Does the user know when the answer is correct or incorrect?
- Is feedback provided to reinforce correct questions?
- Does the program monitor what a child has done and the levels he or she has achieved?
- Can teachers set activity levels for a child to work on when the child can then access them when connected?
- Is there enough content so that children do not have the same question twice? Are the questions random?

6. **Installation**
   ○ During the first installation, did the software install well?
   ○ If not here's a new product just for you!
   ○ Are there known errors with other programs?
   ○ Did it change the configuration of the machine (and leave it that way after use)?
   ○ Can you uninstall the program?

4.4   ISO/IEC 25010[11]

Modeling the quality of the software, it is proper to analyze it in features and sub-features in order to be able to determine the needs and goals of all those interested in the software.

Describing content and evaluating software is a key quality assurance to those interested, who can be either developers, users or buyers of a software, which can be done by defining the necessary and desirable quality features related to their goals. interested members. These quality features are related to the data and the impact that the software has on those interested.

For this purpose, the model was developed ISO/IEC 25010 which is part of the SQuaRE[12] series of international standards.

The model consists of two models that are analyzed below, the Use Quality Model and the Product Quality Model.

Product Quality Model
The quality model is the cornerstone of a product quality assessment system, as it determines what quality features will be taken into account when evaluating the properties of a software product. Thus, when talking about the quality of a system, people refer to the degree to which the system meets the defined and self-evident needs of its various stakeholders and thus provides value. The needs of the interested parties (functionality, performance, safety, maintenance, etc.) are exactly what is represented in the quality model, which categorizes the quality of the product into features and sub-features.

The product quality model defined in the ISO/IEC 25010 standard includes the eight quality characteristics presented in the following figure:

• Functional Suitability represents the degree to which a product or system provides functions that meet defined and self-evident needs when used under specified conditions. This feature consists of the following features:

   a. *Functional completeness.* The degree to which the set of functions covers all defined tasks and user goals.

   b. *Functional correctness.* The degree to which a product or system provides the correct results with the required degree of accuracy.

   c. *Functional appropriateness.* The degree to which functions facilitate the completion of specific tasks and objectives.

---

[11] https://www.iso.org/standard/35733.html

[12] https://iso25000.com/index.php/en/iso-25000-standardsISO/IEC%2025010

- Performance efficiency refers to the extent to which performance is related to the amount of resources used under specified conditions. This feature consists of the following characteristics:

  a. *Time behavior.* The degree to which the response and processing times and the performance rates of a product or system, when performing its functions, meet the requirements.

  b. *Resource utilization.* The extent to which the use of resources from a product or system, when performing its processes, meets the requirements.

  c. *Capacity.* The degree to which the maximum parameters of the product or system meet the requirements.

- Compatibility refers to the extent to which a product, system, or item can exchange information with other products, systems, or components, and/ or perform its required functions while using the same computer or software environment. This feature consists of the following features:

  a. *Co-existence.* The degree to which a product can effectively perform its required functions while sharing a common environment and resources with other products, without having a detrimental effect on any other product.

  b. *Interoperability.* The degree to which two or more systems, products or components can exchange information and use the information exchanged.

- Usability refers to the extent to which a product or system can be used by specific users to achieve specific goals with effectiveness, efficiency, and satisfaction in a particular user context. This feature consists of the following features[13]:

  a. *Appropriateness recognizability.* A level at which users can identify if a product or system is appropriate for their needs.

  b. *Learnability.* The degree to which a product or system can be used by specific users to achieve specific learning objectives using the product or system effectively, risk relief and satisfaction in a particular context.

  c. *Operability.* The degree to which a product or system has features that make it easy to operate, operate, and suitable for use.

  d. *User error protection.* The degree to which a system prevents users from making mistakes.

  e. *User Interface Aesthetics.* The degree to which a user interface allows pleasant and satisfying interaction for the user.

  f. *Accessibility.* The degree to which a product or system can be used by the majority to achieve a specific goal in a defined user context.

- Reliability refers to the extent to which a system, product, or department performs specific functions under specified conditions for a specified period of time. This feature consists of the following characteristics[14]:

---

[13] https://iso25000.com/index.php/en/iso-25000-standards/iso-25010

[14] https://iso25000.com/index.php/en/iso-25000-standards/iso-25010

a. *Maturity.* The degree to which the system, product or department meets the reliability specifications under normal operating conditions.

b. *Availability.* The degree to which a system, product or department is functional and accessible when required for use.

c. *Fault tolerance.* The degree to which a system, product, or department operates as intended, despite the presence of hardware or software errors.

d. *Recoverability.* The degree to which, in the event of interruption or failure, a product or system may recover the affected data and restore the desired state of the system.

- Security refers to the extent to which a product or system protects information and data so that users or other products or systems have adequate access to data depending on the types and levels of licensing. This feature consists of the following characteristics[15]:

a. *Confidentiality.* The degree to which a product or system ensures that data is accessible only to those authorized to access it.

b. *Integrity.* The degree to which a system, product or item prevents unauthorized access or modification of computer programs or data.

c. *Non-repudiation.* The extent to which actions or events can be proven so that events or actions cannot be ruled out later.

d. *Accountability.* The degree to which the actions of an entity can be detected in a unique way in the entity.

e. *Authenticity.* The degree to which the identity of an object or a resource can be proved.

- Maintainability represents the degree to which a system or product can be maintained efficiently and effectively. This feature consists of the following characteristics:

a. *Modularity.* The degree to which a computer system or program consists of separate sections, so that the change in one item has little effect on other items.

b. *Reusability.* The degree to which an element can be used in more than one system or in the construction of other elements.

c. *Analyzability.* The extent to which the impact that a product or system will have on a possible change, in one or more parts, can be evaluated efficiently and effectively, or a product can be diagnosed for deficiencies or causes of errors, or to identify parts that are needed. amendment.

d. *Modifiability.* The degree to which a product or system can be modified efficiently and effectively without entering errors or degrading existing software quality.

e. *Testability.* The degree of efficiency and effectiveness with which the test criteria for a system, product or department and the tests can be determined to determine whether these criteria have been met.

---

[15] https://iso25000.com/index.php/en/iso-25000-standards/iso-25010

- Portability refers to the degree of efficiency and effectiveness with which a system or product can be transferred from one hardware, software or another operating system to another. This feature consists of the following characteristics[16]:

  a. *Adaptability.* The degree to which a product or system can be effectively and efficiently adapted to different or new departments, software or other operating systems.

  b. *Ability to install.* The degree of effectiveness and efficiency with which a product or system can be successfully installed and/or uninstalled in a specified environment.

  c. *Replaceability.* The degree to which a product can replace another specific software product for the same purpose in the same environment.

Quality in Use Model

Quality in use is the degree to which a product or system can be used by specific users to meet their needs to achieve specific goals with effectiveness, efficiency, satisfaction, freedom from risk and satisfaction in specific user environments.

Quality properties during use are categorized into five characteristics: efficiency, effectiveness, satisfaction, error proneness.

- Effectiveness refers to the accuracy and completeness with which users achieve specific goals.
- Efficiency refers to the resources expended in relation to the accuracy and completeness with which users achieve their goals.
- Satisfaction refers to the degree to which user needs are met when a product or system is used in a particular user context.

  a. *Usefulness.* The degree to which the user is satisfied with the results obtained of his realistic goals, including the results and the consequences of use.

  b. *Trust.* The degree to which a user or other interested party considers that a product will have the expected behavior.

  c. *Pleasure.* The degree to which the user is satisfied based on his/her personal needs.

  d. *Comfort.* The degree to which the user is satisfied with physical comfort.

- Freedom from Risk refers to the extent to which a product or system mitigates the potential economic risk to quality of life, health, or the environment.

  a. *Economic Risk Mitigation.* The degree to which a product or system mitigates the potential risk of financial condition, performance, commercial property, reputation or other resources within the intended use framework.

  b. *Health and Safety Risk Mitigation.* The degree to which a product or system mitigates the potential risk to people in the intended context of use.

  c. *Environmental Risk Mitigation.* The degree to which a product or system mitigates the potential risk to property or the environment in the intended use context.

---

[16] https://iso25000.com/index.php/en/iso-25000-standards/iso-25010

- The Context Coverage refers to the degree to which a product or system can be used effectively, efficiently, without risks and with satisfaction in the intended contexts of use and in contexts beyond those originally identified.

    a. *Context Completeness.* The degree to which a product or system can be used effectively, efficiently, without risks and satisfactorily within the intended use frameworks. (for example, the degree to which software can be used using a small screen, with a low network bandwidth, by a non-expert user, and in error-resistant mode (e.g. non-network connectivity).

    b. *Flexibility.* The degree to which a product or system can be used effectively, efficiently, without risks and satisfactorily in environments beyond those originally defined in the requirements.

- Some of these features and sub-features of the ISO/IEC 25010 standard, which are related to the evaluation frameworks, we will use below to compare the evaluation frames recorded above.

4.5   Comparison of Evaluation Frameworks

Table 5.

ISO/IEC25010	Evaluation Framework for Use of Uses				Evaluation Framework for Educational Applications							
	RITA	Four levels of Kirkpatrick	CIAO	Five level ROI	The five levels of Kaufman Assessment	Anderson Learning Value Model	Brinkerhoff Success Case Method	Four Dimensions (FDF)	SECAL	Hubbard evaluation framework	Chappelle evaluation framework	M3
Product Quality Model												
Operating Completion												
Functional completeness	X	X	X	X	X			X			X	X
Functional correctness	X	X	X	X	X		X	X	X			X
Functional suitability	X	X	X	X	X	X	X	X		X	X	X
Execution of Execution												
Chronic behavior	X											
Use of resources					X	X			X			X
Compatibility												
Coexistence	X	X										
Interoperability	X											
Usability												
Recognition of suitability	X	X	X	X	X		X	X	X		X	X
Learning ability	X	X	X	X	X		X	X	X		X	X

Table 5. Contined.

ISO/IEC25010	Evaluation Framework for Use of Uses	Evaluation Framework for Educational Applications										
	RITA	Four levels of Kirkpatrick	CIAO	Five level ROI	The five levels of Kaufman Assessment	Anderson Learning Value Model	Brinkerhoff Success Case Method	Four Dimensions (FDF)	SECAL	Hubbard evaluation framework	Chappelle evaluation framework	M3
Handling	X	X	X	X		X		X	X	X		X
Aesthetics of the user interface	X											
Accessibility	X	X	X	X		X		X	X	X	X	X
Reliability												
Maturity	X	X	X	X	X		X	X	X		X	X
Availability	X											
Possibility of Maintenance												
Sectionality	X											
Reuse								X	X	X		
Detailed			X				X	X		X		X
Possibility of modification							X			X	X	X
Possibility to test		X		X			X	X	X			X
Portability												
Adaptability	X	X	X	X	X	X	X	X	X	X		

Table 5. Contined.

ISO/IEC25010	Evaluation Framework for Use of Uses				Evaluation Framework for Educational Applications							
	RITA	Four levels of Kirkpatrick	CIAO	Five level ROI	The five levels of Kaufman Assessment	Anderson Learning Value Model	Brinkerhoff Success Case Method	Four Dimensions (FDF)	SECAL	Hubbard evaluation framework	Chappelle evaluation framework	M3
Possibility of replacement		X	X	X	X	X	X	X	X		X	X
Model of Use Quality												
Effectiveness	X	X	X	X	X		X	X	X		X	X
Efficiency	X	X		X	X		X	X				X
Satisfaction												
Usefulness	X	X	X	X	X		X	X	X		X	X
Confidence	X						X				X	
Freedom from Risks												
Financial risk mitigation		X	X	X	X	X	X					
Mitigation of health and safety risk							X					
Mitigation of environmental risk					X	X	X					
Cover Framework												
Fulfillment framework	X	X	X	X	X		X	X	X			X
Elasticity		X								X		X

Table 6.

ISO/IEC25010	Evaluation Framework for Personal Systems		Evaluation Framework for Educational Games						
	EFEx	Assessment Framework for Adaptive Supplements (Arpita Gupta, PS Grover)	Pre-MEGa	PLU-E	Methodological framework for the evaluation of educational games (A. Antoniou, D. Diakakis, G. Lepouras, K. Vasilakis)	GOM II	Assessment framework for learning based on games (Conolly, Stansfield and Hainey, 2007, de Freitas, 2006)	RETAIN	TEEM
Product Quality Model									
Operating Completion									
Functional completeness	X	X		X	X			X	
Functional correctness	X	X	X	X	X		X	X	X
Functional suitability	X	X	X			X	X	X	X
Execution of Execution									
Chronic behavior	X			X	X			X	
Use of resources	X	X		X				X	
Compatibility									
Coexistence									
Interoperability	X	X							
Christicity									
Recognition of suitability	X	X	X	X	X	X		X	
Learning ability	X	X		X	X	X	X	X	X
Handling	X		X	X	X	X		X	X

Table 6. Contined.

ISO/IEC25010	Evaluation Framework for Personal Systems		Evaluation Framework for Educational Games			
	EFEx	Pre-MEGa — Assessment Framework for Adaptive Supplements (Arpita Gupta, PS Grover)	PLU-E	GOM II — Methodological framework for the evaluation of educational games (A. Antoniou, D. Diakakis, G. Lepouras, K. Vasilakis)	RETAIN — Assessment framework for learning based on games (Conolly, Stansfield and Hainey, 2007, de Freitas, 2006)	TEEM
Aesthetics of the user interface	X					
Accessibility	X			X	X	X
Reliability						
Maturity	X	X	X	X	X	
Availability	X		X			
Possibility of Maintenance						
Sectionality		X			X	
Reuse		X				
Detailed			X	X		
Possibility of modification		X				
Possibility to test						
Portability						
Adaptability	X			X	X	
Possibility of replacement		X	X	X	X	X

Table 6. Continued.

ISO/IEC25010	Evaluation Framework for Personal Systems		Evaluation Framework for Educational Games						
	EFEx	Assessment Framework for Adaptive Supplements (Arpita Gupta, PS Grover)	Pre-MEGa	PLU-E	Methodological framework for the evaluation of educational games (A. Antoniou, D. Diakakis, G. Lepouras, K. Vasilakis)	GOM II	Assessment framework for learning based on games (Conolly, Stansfield and Hainey, 2007, de Freitas, 2006)	RETAIN	TEEM
Model of Use Quality									
Effectiveness	X	X						X	
Efficiency	X		X	X	X		X	X	X
Satisfaction									
Usefulness	X	X	X	X	X	X		X	
Confidence	X	X							
Freedom from Risks									
Financial risk mitigation									
Mitigation of health and safety risk									
Mitigation of environmental risk									
Cover Framework									
Fulfillment framework	X	X	X	X	X	X		X	X
Elasticity					X			X	

Observing the above tables, we distinguish the qualitative results of the evaluation of the specific evaluation frameworks, based on the quality standard ISO/IEC 25010. This helps us to draw some conclusions about these frameworks individually and as a whole.

Looking at the tables, it is inferred that some features are used in most, if not all, frameworks. These are: adaptability and replacement capability (as it is very important for a framework to both be able to adapt efficiently and effectively to different environments, and to be able to replace another framework for the same purpose), the functional correctness, (since what we mainly ask of an evaluation framework is to provide us with the most accurate and correct results possible, the functional suitability (that is, how much the specific framework makes it easier for us to achieve the tasks and our goals), the learning ability and handling of a framework, maturity (to meet the reliability requirements). Efficiency, effectiveness and usefulness of the evaluation frameworks also play a significant role.

Judging by the amount of quality features of a frame, then we will conclude that the best evaluation frameworks are the EFEx and SC of Brinkenhoff. EFEx outperforms Birkenhoff in performance, in contrast to SC which outperforms financial risk mitigation and freedom from risk in general. Both are very important parameters of a framework because the ultimate result is the profit in a business or an organization that uses the specific frameworks. Also, SC excels in the ability to modify and replace, as it can be modified and customized according to the user's needs, but it can also replace another product for a similar purpose. On the contrary, the TEEM and the Hubbard evaluation frameworks, although holding some key features, such as functional suitability, accessibility or handling, have a disadvantage over the rest regarding functional completeness, suitability recognition, maturity or effectiveness.

Taking into account the categories of the frameworks, we come to other conclusions. For example, one of the best assessment frameworks for educational applications is Kirkpatrick's four-level assessment framework, Jones' CIAO, and Birkenhoff's SC as they have characteristics that are particularly important for the purpose they serve, such as accessibility, handling, suitability recognition, learning ability and financial risk mitigation, being one of the most important results of the efficient and effective use of these frameworks.

Therefore, the perspective changes if we do the same for the evaluation frameworks mentioned in the educational games. In this area we can say that the RETAIN model prevails in several features compared to the rest of its class. Some of these are time-consuming behavior and the use of resources that contribute to the performance of the framework, accessibility, as it can be used by the majority of users to achieve the evaluation of an educational game, segmentation, as it is particularly useful feature maintenance of a product and efficiency, which is undoubtedly a point of excellence for any category of frame.

In terms of adaptive systems evaluation frameworks, we can see some significant differences in the two recorded frameworks. Starting with time behavior, one of the features that give EFEx a significant lead, as time is a very critical factor not only in this category, but in general. Another sub-feature that prevails in EFEx is the adaptability that is particularly useful for a framework as it can be effectively and efficiently adapted to different software in the same category and the efficiency of this framework, compared to the proposed framework for adaptive media, which in turn outperforms the sub-features of maintenance capability, which is particularly useful, which helps to partially balance their difference.

One category that cannot be left out is that of user evaluation interfaces, which in this dissertation have been recorded in a single context, although there are generally many more in the literature. The RITA evaluation framework is clear from the comparison table, that it is included in the context with most features and sub-features of the ISO/IEC 25010 standard. This is because it is considered an adjustable frame, as it has a modular architecture that can be configured to evaluate different user interfaces. So having the feature of segmentation, based on the quality standard, consists of four units, which collect, manage and analyze the data for the evaluation of a system, and a change in one of them has little effect on the others. In addition, RITA is not only a general framework for evaluating various interaction systems, but also has the feature of functional suitability, which is very important for any category of framework, as it facilitates the achievement of user goals by providing accurate and precise results.

From the above observations, we could conclude that there is not a perfect model and framework neither if we see them as parts of the specific categories recorded, nor in general. That means that the selection of the appropriate model needs to be aligned to the kind of software that will be evaluated. Everything has advantages and disadvantages over others but everything can be used for its own purpose providing the right results for its operation.

Chapter 5:
Conclusions

Artificial intelligence has already been applied to education, especially in some tools developing educational software. By leveraging the best features of artificial intelligence techniques, the vision for artificial intelligence in education will provide the best possible outcome for students' educational progress. Using educational software based on artificial intelligence can significantly improve the effectiveness of many educational processes. Artificial intelligence can render teachers capable of providing a greater picture of students' needs and preferences.

Knowledge-based approaches in the field of e-learning can have considerable improvements in this rapidly growing research field. Both instructors and students can be supported by these novel advancements and can then be able to reap the benefits of a personalized and adaptive learning technology system.

With regard to smart architectures used in e-learning, it can be said that there is a basic level of application. Its main goal is to personalize the learning of each user according to his/her needs and the interactions that all students experienced during the learning process.

As mentioned, artificial intelligence has intruded our everyday life and as such people should consider the considerable changes that this field offers. Specifically, in e-learning, students can interact in an environment that can make predictions and diagnosis of their actions towards enhancing the pedagogical and technological affordance of their experience.

Regarding smart e-learning architectures, the main future direction is the fully automatic adaptation of the learning flow, depending on the movements of each user.

Additional topics that can be considered are the multiple models of recording the educational flow of the same learner, the training process based on time reports as well as micro/macro-long-term educational potential.

Another ongoing debate about the use of artificial intelligence needs to be made. Given that technology is changing, parallel changes pertaining to customs, policies, social acceptance and the economy must also be conducted. The effects of artificial intelligence show that there is a great need for skills as the environment develops rapidly and the education system needs to adapt to these changes, especially when it comes to skills development. Artificial intelligence helps the automation of many of the productive processes that were previously done by humans. So, as artificial intelligence improves processes, perhaps it would be necessary to redesign educational institutions/organizations.

Artificial intelligence provides new means of research in education, but it is also important to consider the capabilities of systems when using information/knowledge about the educational process. Software designers and tutors of the educational process can provide much more information on how to better match artificial intelligence and education both in the educational context and in other areas of application.

References

Aajli, A. and K. Afdel, "Generation of an adaptive e-learning domain model based on a fuzzy logic approach," 2016 IEEE/ACS 13th International Conference of Computer Systems and Applications (AICCSA), Agadir, 2016, pp. 1-8, doi: 10.1109/AICCSA.2016.7945708.

Ahlberg, C. and Shneiderman, B. (1994). Visual information seeking: tight coupling of dynamic query filters with starfield displays, CHI 94 Boston. (pp. 313-317). New York: ACM.

Alharbi, M. and Jemmali, M., 2017. Artificial Intelligent e-Learning Architecture. *Ninth International Conference on Machine Vision (ICMV 2016), 103412G,* p. Proc. SPIE 10341.

Alonso, F., López, G., Manrique, D. and Viñes, J. M., 2005. An instructional model for web-based e-learning education with a blended learning process approach. *British Journal of Educational Technology, 36(2),* pp. 217-235.

Amory, A., Game object model version II: a theoretical framework for educational game development. Education Tech Research Dev 55, 51–77 (2007). https://doi.org/10.1007/s11423-006-9001-x.

Antoniou, Angeliki, Dimitris Diakakis, George Lepouras and Costas Vasilakis, Towards a methodological framework for the cognitive-behavioural evaluation of educational e-games, International Journal of Learning Technology (IJLT), Vol. 6, No. 3, 2011.

Arriaga, F. de, M. El Alami and A. Arriaga, Evaluation of Fuzzy Intelligent Learning Systems, Recent Research Developments in Learning Technologies, 2005, pp. 1-5.

Bai, S. M. and Chen, S. M. (2008). Automatically constructing concept maps based on fuzzy rules for adapting learning systems. Expert systems with Applications, 35(1), 41-49.

Barros, B. and Verdejo, M.F., (2000). Analysing student interaction processes in order to improve collaboration. The DEGREE approach. International Journal of Artificial Intelligence in Education, 11, pp. 221-241.

Bhutto, E. S., I. F. Siddiqui, Q. A. Arain and M. Anwar, "Predicting Students' Academic Performance Through Supervised Machine Learning," 2020 International Conference on Information Science and Communication Technology (ICISCT), KARACHI, Pakistan, 2020, pp. 1-6, doi: 10.1109/ICISCT49550.2020.9080033.

Calvary, G., Coutaz J., Thevenin, D., Limbourg, Q., Bouillon, L. and Vanderdonckt, J., A unifying reference framework for multi-target user interfaces, Interacting With Computers, Vol. 15/3, 2003, pp 289-308.

Chapelle, C. (2001). Computer applications in second language acquisition: Foundations for teaching, testing and research. Cambridge: Cambridge University Press.

Charfi, S., H. Ezzedine and C. Kolski, "RITA: A framework based on multi-evaluation techniques for user interface evaluation: Application to a transport network supervision system," 2013 International Conference on Advanced Logistics and Transport, Sousse, 2013, pp. 263-268, doi: 10.1109/ICAdLT.2013.6568470.

Cheng, C.Y.Y. and J. Yen, "Virtual Learning Environment (VLE): a Web-based collaborative learning system," Proceedings of the Thirty-First Hawaii International Conference on System Sciences, Kohala Coast, HI, USA, 1998, pp. 480-491 vol.1, doi: 10.1109/HICSS.1998.653133.

Chrysafiadi, Konstantina, Christos Troussas, Maria Virvou and Evangelos Sakkopoulos, ICALM: an Intelligent Mechanism for the Creation of Dynamically Adaptive Learning Material, Sensors & Transducers Journal, Vol. 234, Issue 6, June 2019, pp. 22-29.

Chu, R.W., C. M. Mitchell and P. M. Jones, "Using the operator function model and OFMspert as the basis for an intelligent tutoring system: towards a tutor/aid paradigm for operators of supervisory control systems," in IEEE Transactions on Systems, Man and Cybernetics, vol. 25, no. 7, pp. 1054-1075, July 1995, doi: 10.1109/21.391287.

Connolly, T.M., E. A. Boyle, E. MacArthur, T. Hainey and J. M. Boyle, "A systematic literature review of empirical evidence on computer games and serious games", Comput. Educ., vol. 59, no. 2, pp. 661-686, 2012.

Damez, M., Dang, T. H., Marsala, C. and Bouchon-Meunier, B. (2005, November). Fuzzy decision tree for user modeling from human-computer interactions. In: Proceedings of the 5th International Conference on Human System Learning, ICHSL, Vol. 5, pp. 287-302.

De Freitas, S., Rebolledo-Mendez, G., Liarokapis, F., Magoulas, G. and Poulovassilis, A. (2010), Learning as immersive experiences: Using the four-dimensional framework for designing and evaluating immersive learning experiences in a virtual world. British Journal of Educational Technology, 41: 69-85.

Dix, A., Talis, Human-Like Computing and Human–Computer Interaction, Proceedings of the 30th International BCS Human Computer Interaction Conference, 2016.

Dugdale, J., Pallamin, N. and Pavard, B. (2006). An assessment of a mixed reality environment: Toward an ethnomethodological approach. Simulation & Gaming, 37(2), 226–244. https://doi.org/10.1177/1046878105284450.

Duhayyim, Mesfer Al and Paul Newbury, Concept-based and Fuzzy Adaptive E-learning, Proceedings of the 2018 The 3rd International Conference on Information and Education Innovations, June 2018, Pages 49–56, https://doi.org/10.1145/3234825.3234832.

Fazlollahtabar, Hamed and Mahdavi, Iraj, User/Tutor Optimal Learning Path in E-Learning Using Comprehensive Neuro-Fuzzy Approach, Educational Research Review, v4 n2 p142-155 2009.

Firte, A.A., C. V. Bratu and C. Cenan, "Intelligent component for adaptive E-learning systems," 2009 IEEE 5th International Conference on Intelligent Computer Communication and Processing, Cluj-Napoca, 2009, pp. 35-38, doi: 10.1109/ICCP.2009.5284788.

Fu, D., R. Jensen and E. Hinkelman, "Evaluating Game Technologies for Training," 2008 IEEE Aerospace Conference, Big Sky, MT, 2008, pp. 1-10, doi: 10.1109/AERO.2008.4526579.

Gackenbach, J. and M. Rosie, Cognitive evaluation of video games: players' perceptions, Future Play '09: Proceedings of the 2009 Conference on Future Play on @ GDC Canada, May 2009, Pages 23–24.

Gazzard, A., "The Avatar and the Player: Understanding the Relationship beyond the Screen," 2009 Conference in Games and Virtual Worlds for Serious Applications, Coventry, 2009, pp. 190-193, doi: 10.1109/VS-GAMES.2009.11.

Greer, J., 1995. *World Conference on Artificial Intelligence in Education.* s.l., Assocaition for Advancement of Computing in Education (AACE).

Gunn, C. (1997) CAL evaluation: Future directions, ALT-J, 5:1, 40-47, DOI: 10.1080/0968776970050107.

Gunter, G.A., Kenny, R.F. and Vick, E.H. Taking educational games seriously: using the RETAIN model to design endogenous fantasy into standalone educational games. Education Tech Research Dev 56, 511–537 (2008). https://doi.org/10.1007/s11423-007-9073-2

Gupta, A.D. and Grover, P.S. (2004). Proposed Evaluation Framework for Adaptive Hypermedia Systems.

Hawkes, L. W. and Derry, S. J. (1996). Advances in local student modeling using informal fuzzy reasoning. International Journal of Human–Computer Studies, 45, 697–722.

Hawkes, L. W., Derry, S. J. and Rundensteiner, E. A. (1990). Individualized tutoring using an intelligent fuzzy temporal relational database. International Journal of Man–Machines Studies, 33, 409–429.

Hendaoui, A., M. Limayem and C. W. Thompson, "3D Social Virtual Worlds: Research Issues and Challenges," in IEEE Internet Computing, vol. 12, no. 1, pp. 88-92, Jan.-Feb. 2008, doi: 10.1109/MIC.2008.1.

Hogo, Mofreh A., Evaluation of E-Learners Behaviour using Different Fuzzy Clustering Models: A Comparative Study, International Journal of Computer Science and Information Security, IJCSIS, Vol. 7 No. 2, February 2010.

Hsieh, T. C., Wang, T. I., Su, C. Y. and Lee, M. C. (2012). A Fuzzy Logic-based Personalized Learning System for Supporting Adaptive English Learning. Educational Technology & Society, 15(1), 273-288.

Hubbard, P. (2011). Evaluation of courseware and websites. In L. Ducate and N. Arnold (Eds.), Present and future promises of CALL: From theory and research to new directions in foreign language teaching (pp. 407-440). San Marcos, TX: CALICO.

Isiaka, R.M., E.O. Omidiora, S.O. Olabiyisi and O.O. Okediran, An Enhanced Learning Technology System Architecture for Web-Based Instructional Design, iJET – Volume 11, Issue 1, 2016.

Ivory, M. and M. Hearst, The state of the art in automating usability evaluation of user interfaces, ACM Computing Surveys, December 2001.

Jameson, A., Numerical uncertainty management in user and student modeling: An overview of systems and issues. User Model User-Adap Inter 5, 193–251 (1995). https://doi.org/10.1007/BF01126111.

Jones, A., Scanlon, E., Tosunoglu, C., Morris, E., Ross, S., Butcher, P. and Greenberg, J., "Contexts for evaluating educational software", Interacting with Computers, 11(5), pp. 499–516, 1999.

Karna, N., "New model of e-learning based on knowledge management system," 2017 2nd International conferences on Information Technology, Information Systems and Electrical Engineering (ICITISEE), Yogyakarta, 2017, pp. 7-10, doi: 10.1109/ICITISEE.2017.8285562.

Katoua, H. S., 2012. Reasoning Methodologies for Intelligent e-Learning Systems. International Journal of Computing Academic Research, 1(1), pp. 36-44.

Kirkpatrick, Donald L. "Techniques for evaluating training programs." (1979).

Koohang, A. and Harman, K., 2005. Open source: A metaphor for e-learning. *Informing Science Journal, 8,* pp. 75-86.

Krouska, A., C. Troussas and M. Virvou, "Social networks as a learning environment: Developed applications and comparative analysis," 2017 8th International Conference on Information, Intelligence, Systems & Applications (IISA), Larnaca, 2017, pp. 1-6, doi: 10.1109/IISA.2017.8316430.

Krouska, A., C. Troussas, M. Virvou and C. K. Fragkakis, "Applying Skinnerian Conditioning for Shaping Skill Performance in Online Tutoring of Programming Languages," 2018 9th International Conference on Information, Intelligence, Systems and Applications (IISA), Zakynthos, Greece, 2018, pp. 1-5, doi: 10.1109/IISA.2018.8633614.

Krouska, A., C. Troussas and M. Virvou, "Using Learning Analytics to Improve the Efficacy of Mobile Authoring Tools," 2019 10th International Conference on Information, Intelligence, Systems and Applications (IISA), PATRAS, Greece, 2019, pp. 1-5, doi: 10.1109/IISA.2019.8900726. (a)

Krouska, Akrivi, Troussas, Christos and Virvou, Maria. 'Applying Genetic Algorithms for Student Grouping in Collaborative Learning: A Synthetic Literature Review'. 1 Jan. 2019 : 395 – 406. (b)

Krouska, Akrivi, Christos Troussas and Cleo Sgouropoulou, Fuzzy Logic for Refining the Evaluation of Learners' Performance in Online Engineering Education, European Journal of Engineering Research and Science (EJERS), Vol. 4, No. 6, June 2019. (c)

Krouska A., Troussas C. and Sgouropoulou C. (2020), Applying Genetic Algorithms for Recommending Adequate Competitors in Mobile Game-Based Learning Environments. In: Kumar V., Troussas C. (eds) Intelligent Tutoring Systems. ITS 2020. Lecture Notes in Computer Science, vol 12149. Springer, Cham

Lascio, Luigi Di, Antonio Gisolfi and Vincenzo Loia, Uncertainty processing in user-modeling activity, Information Sciences, Volume 106, Issues 1–2, 1998, Pages 25-47.

Lau, R. Y. K., D. Song, Y. Li, T. C. H. Cheung and J. Hao, "Toward a Fuzzy Domain Ontology Extraction Method for Adaptive e-Learning," in IEEE Transactions on Knowledge and Data Engineering, vol. 21, no. 6, pp. 800-813, June 2009, doi: 10.1109/TKDE.2008.137.

Lee, S. H., J. Choi and J. Park, "Interactive e-learning system using pattern recognition and augmented reality," in IEEE Transactions on Consumer Electronics, vol. 55, no. 2, pp. 883-890, May 2009, doi: 10.1109/TCE.2009.5174470.

Leutner, D. (2000), Double-fading support — a training approach to complex software systems. Journal of Computer Assisted Learning, 16: 347-357. doi:10.1046/j.1365-2729.2000.00147.x

Liarokapis, F., Mourkoussis, N., White, M., Darcy, J., Sifniotis, M., Petridis, P., Basu, A. and Lister, P.F. (2004). Web3D and Augmented Reality to support Engineering Education, World Transactions on Engineering and Technology Education, 3(1), 2004.

MacDonald, C. and M. Artwood, What does it mean for a system to be useful?: an exploratory study of usefulness, Proceedings of the 2014 conference on Designing interactive systems, June 2014, Pages 885–894.

Malone, T.W., What makes things fun to learn? heuristics for designing instructional computer games, SIGSMALL '80: Proceedings of the 3rd ACM SIGSMALL symposium and the first SIGPC symposium on Small systems, September 1980 Pages 162–169.

McAllister, K. (2004). Game work. Language, power and computer game culture. Tuscaloosa: The University of Alabama Press.

Meacham, S., D. Nauck and H. Zhao, "Framework for Personalised Online Education based on Learning Analytics through the use of Domain-Specific Modelling and Data Analytics," 2019 Conference on Next Generation Computing Applications (NextComp), Mauritius, 2019, pp. 1-7, doi: 10.1109/NEXTCOMP.2019.8883640.

Mihalis P. and Maria G. (1995) An application of fuzzy logic to student modelling. In: Tinsley J.D., van Weert T.J. (eds) World Conference on Computers in Education VI. WCCE 1995. IFIP – The International Federation for Information Processing. Springer, Boston, MA.

Monova-Zheleva, M., Zhelev, Y., and Mascitti, I. (2008). E-Learning, e-Practising and e-Tutoring: an Integrated Approach, Methodologies and Tools of the Modern (e-) Learning, pp. 84-90.

Mota, J., Using learning styles and neural networks as an approach to elearning content and layout adaptation. In Doctoral Symposium on Informatics Engineering, 2008.

Mulwa, Catherine, Seamus Lawless, Mary Sharp and Vincent Wade, An Evaluation Framework for End-User Experience in Adaptive Systems, User Modeling, Adaptation and Personalization Conference (UMAP), Girona, Spain, 11th 15th July, 2011.

Myszkorowski, K. and Zakrzewska, D. (2013). Using fuzzy logic for recommending groups in e-learning systems. In Computational Collective Intelligence. Technologies and Applications (pp. 671-680). Springer Berlin Heidelberg.

Park, Hyungjoo and Song, Hae-Deok, Make E-Learning Effortless! Impact of a Redesigned User Interface on Usability through the Application of an Affordance Design Approach, Educational Technology & Society, v18 n3 p185-196 2015.

Pestana Santos, F. R., I. de Almeida Souza Concilio and J. Pessoa Filho, "Development of Learning Objects for Teaching Mathematics using SCORM," 2018 XIII Latin American Conference on Learning Technologies (LACLO), São Paulo, Brazil, 2018, pp. 264-269, doi: 10.1109/LACLO.2018.00055.

Prasolova-Førland, E. and Divitini, M. (2003). Collaborative virtual environments for supporting learning communities: An experience of Use. In Proceedings of the ACM GROUP 2003 (pp. 58-67). ACM Press.

Preece, J., Y. Rogers, H. Sharp, D. Benyon, S. Holland and T. Carey, Human-Computer Interaction: Concepts and Design, Pearson Education, 1994.

Rañó, I., "Results on the Convergence of Braitenberg Vehicle 3a," in Artificial Life, vol. 20, no. 2, pp. 223-235, April 2014, doi: 10.1162/ARTL_a_00108.

Rasmani, K. A. and Shen, Q. (2006). Data-driven fuzzy rule generation and its application for student academic performance evaluation. Applied Intelligence, 25, 305–319.

Redondo, M. A., Bravo, C., Bravo, J. and Ortega, M. (2003). Applying fuzzy logic to analyze collaborative learning experiences in an e-learning environment. USDLA Journal. (United States Distance Learning Association), 17, 19-28.

Repčíková, S., "Datafication of education enhancing teaching and learning through data mining and learning analyses," 2013 IEEE 11th International Conference on Emerging eLearning Technologies and Applications (ICETA), Stara Lesna, 2013, pp. 335-338, doi: 10.1109/ICETA.2013.6674454.

Rich, E., Artificial intelligence and the humanities. Comput Hum 19, 117–122 (1985). https://doi.org/10.1007/BF02259633

Rieber, L. P. (1996). Seriously considering play: Designing interactive learning environments based on the blending of microworlds, simulations and games. Educational Technology Research & Development, 44(2), 43-58.

Salem, A.-B. M., 2010. Ontological Engineering in e-Learning. *8th International Conference on Emerging e-learning Technologies and Applications, Information and Communication Technologies in Learning, (ICETA2010)*.

Sangrà, A., Vlachopoulos, D. and Cabrera, N., 2012. Building an Inclusive Definition of E-Learning: An Approach to the Conceptual Framework. *International Review of Research in Open and Distance Learning, 13(2)*, pp. 145-159.

Senach, B. (1990). Evaluation ergonomique des interfaces homme-machine: une revue de la littérature. Rapport de recherche INRIA-Sophia Antipolis, Mars 1990.

Sharma, K., Sood, D., Singh, A. and Pandit, P., 2010. Strategic architecture for e-learning at HP University. *International Journal of Educational Management, vol. 24, no. 7*, pp. 575-596.

Shoukry, L., Sturm, C. and Galal-Edeen, G.H. (2015) Pre-MEGa: A Proposed Framework for the Design and Evaluation of Preschoolers' Mobile Educational Games. In: Sobh T., Elleithy K. (eds) Innovations and Advances in Computing, Informatics, Systems Sciences, Networking and Engineering. Lecture Notes in Electrical Engineering, vol 313. Springer, Cham.

Shute, V. J. and Zapata-Rivera, D., 2012. Adaptive educational systems. In: *Adaptive Technologies for Training and Education.* New York: Cambridge University Press, pp. 7-27.

Stathacopoulou, R., G. D. Magoulas and M. Grigoriadou, "Neural network-based fuzzy modeling of the student in intelligent tutoring systems," IJCNN'99. International Joint Conference on Neural Networks. Proceedings (Cat. No.99CH36339), Washington, DC, USA, 1999, pp. 3517-3521 vol.5, doi: 10.1109/IJCNN.1999.836233.

Sue, P. C., Weng, J. F., Su, J. M. and Tseng, S. S. (2004). A new approach for constructing the concept map. In Proceedings of the 2004 IEEE international conference on advanced learning technologies (pp. 76–80).

Tan, A. J. Q., C. C. S. Lau and S. Y. Liaw, "Paper title: Serious games in nursing education: An integrative review," 2017 9th International Conference on Virtual Worlds and Games for Serious Applications (VS-Games), Athens, 2017, pp. 187-188, doi: 10.1109/VS-GAMES.2017.8056599.

Taylor M.J., McNicholas C., Nicolay C. et al, Systematic review of the application of the plan–do–study–act method to improve quality in healthcare, BMJ Quality & Safety 2014;23:290-298.

Troussas, C., M. Virvou, J. Caro and K. J. Espinosa, "Mining relationships among user clusters in Facebook for language learning," 2013 International Conference on Computer, Information and Telecommunication Systems (CITS), Athens, 2013, pp. 1-5, doi: 10.1109/CITS.2013.6705722.

Troussas, C., A. Krouska and M. Virvou, "NLP-based error analysis and dynamic motivation techniques in mobile learning," 2019 10th International Conference on Information, Intelligence, Systems and Applications (IISA), PATRAS, Greece, 2019, pp. 1-8, doi: 10.1109/IISA.2019.8900729. (a)

Troussas, C., A. Krouska and M. Virvou, "Injecting intelligence into learning management systems: The case of adaptive grain-size instruction," 2019 10th International Conference on Information, Intelligence, Systems and Applications (IISA), PATRAS, Greece, 2019, pp. 1-6, doi: 10.1109/IISA.2019.8900779. (b)

Troussas, C., A. Krouska and M. Virvou, "Adaptive e-learning interactions using dynamic clustering of learners' characteristics," 2019 10th International Conference on Information, Intelligence, Systems and Applications (IISA), PATRAS, Greece, 2019, pp. 1-7, doi: 10.1109/IISA.2019.8900722. (c)

Troussas, Christos, Konstantina Chrysafiadi, Maria Virvou, An intelligent adaptive fuzzy-based inference system for computer-assisted language learning, Expert Systems with Applications, Volume 127, 2019, Pages 85-96. (d)

Troussas, Christos, Filippos Giannakas, Cleo Sgouropoulou and Ioannis Voyiatzis (2020) Collaborative activities recommendation based on students' collaborative learning styles using ANN and WSM, Interactive Learning Environments, DOI: 10.1080/10494820.2020.1761835. (a)

Troussas C., Krouska A. and Virvou M. (2020) Using a Multi Module Model for Learning Analytics to Predict Learners' Cognitive States and Provide Tailored Learning Pathways and Assessment. In: Virvou M., Alepis E., Tsihrintzis G., Jain L. (eds) Machine Learning Paradigms. Intelligent Systems Reference Library, vol 158. Springer, Cham. (b)

Troussas, C., Krouska, A. and Sgouropoulou, C. (2020) Dynamic Detection of Learning Modalities Using Fuzzy Logic in Students' Interaction Activities. In: Kumar V., Troussas C. (eds) Intelligent Tutoring Systems. ITS 2020. Lecture Notes in Computer Science, vol 12149. Springer, Cham. (c)

Troussas, Christos, Akrivi Krouska and Cleo Sgouropoulou, Collaboration and fuzzy-modeled personalization for mobile game-based learning in higher education. Computers & Education, 144 (2020). (d)

Tsai, C. J., Tseng, S. S. and Lin, C. Y. (2001). A two-phase fuzzy mining and learning algorithm for adaptive learning environment. In Proceedings of the international conference on computational science, Lecture notes in computer science (LNCS 2074), California, U.S.A. (Vol. 2, pp. 429–438).

Tseng, S. S., Sue, P. C., Su, J. M., Weng, J. F. and Tsai, W. N. (2007). A new approach for constructing the concept map. Computers & Education, 49(3), 691-707.

Vavoula, G. and Sharples, M. (2009). Meeting the Challenges in Evaluating Mobile Learning: A 3-Level Evaluation Framework. International Journal of Mobile and Blended Learning (IJMBL), 1(2), 54-75. doi:10.4018/jmbl.2009040104.

Virvou, M., E. Alepis and C. Troussas, "User Modeling on Communication Characteristics Using Machine Learning in Computer-Supported Collaborative Multiple Language Learning," 2012 IEEE 24th International Conference on Tools with Artificial Intelligence, Athens, 2012, pp. 1088-1093, doi: 10.1109/ICTAI.2012.154.

Vrettaros J., Vouros G. and Drigas A. (2007) Development of an Intelligent Assessment System for Solo Taxonomies Using Fuzzy Logic. In: Mellouli K. (eds) Symbolic and Quantitative Approaches to Reasoning with Uncertainty. ECSQARU 2007. Lecture Notes in Computer Science, vol 4724. Springer, Berlin, Heidelberg.

Wang, X., H. He, P. Li and L. Zhang, "Research on the Disciplinary Evolution of Deep Learning and the Educational Revelation," 2019 14th International Conference on Computer Science & Education (ICCSE), Toronto, ON, Canada, 2019, pp. 655-660, doi: 10.1109/ICCSE.2019.8845446.

Warendorf, K., and Tsao, S. J. (1997). Application of fuzzy logic techniques in the BSS1 tutoring system. Journal of Artificial Intelligence in Education, 8, 113-146.

Wilson, S. et al., 2007. Personal Learning Environments: challenging the dominant design of educational systems. *Journal of e-Learning and Knowledge Society*, pp. 27-38.

Xu, Dongming, Huaiqing Wang and Kaile Su, "Intelligent student profiling with fuzzy models," Proceedings of the 35th Annual Hawaii International Conference on System Sciences, Big Island, HI, 2002, pp. 8 pp.-, doi: 10.1109/HICSS.2002.994005.

Yang, H. and H. Wu, "The Application of SPOC-Based Deep Learning Model in Psychological Health Education of College Students in Post-MOOC Era," 2019 10th International Conference on Information Technology in Medicine and Education (ITME), Qingdao, China, 2019, pp. 230-233, doi: 10.1109/ITME.2019.00059.

Yu, P., Own, C. and Lin, L., On learning behavior analysis of web based interactive environment, Proceedings of ICCEE, 2001.

Zhang, Z., Basili, V. and Shneiderman, B. Perspective-based Usability Inspection: An Empirical Validation of Efficacy. Empirical Software Engineering 4, 43–69 (1999). https://doi.org/10.1023/A:1009803214692.

Zhou, D., Zhang, Z., Zhong, S. and Xie, P., 2008. The design of software architecture for e-learning platforms. *Technologies for E-Learning and Digital Entertainment Springer*, pp. 32-40.

www.ingramcontent.com/pod-product-compliance
Ingram Content Group UK Ltd.
Pitfield, Milton Keynes, MK11 3LW, UK
UKHW050044180526
471099UK00006B/210